The
Elements
of
Correspondence

Also by the Author

The
Elements
of
Correspondence

MARY A. DE VRIES

Macmillan • USA

MACMILLAN
A Simon & Schuster Macmillan Company
1633 Broadway
New York, NY 10019

Library of Congress Cataloging-in-Publication Data
De Vries, Mary Ann.
    The elements of correspondence / Mary A. De Vries.
        p.   cm.
    Originally published: 1995.
    Includes index.
    ISBN 0-02-860840-2 (pbk.)
    1. Letter writing—Handbooks, manuals, etc. 2. English language—
Rhetoric—Handbooks, manuals, etc. 3. Commercial correspondence—
Handbooks, manuals, etc.   I. Title.
[PE1483.D44   1996]
808.6—dc20   96-1433
                                                       CIP

10 9 8 7 6 5 4 3 2 1

Printed in the United States of America

Contents

Preface

As I finish this, my fifth book about letter writing, it's hard to believe that I once cringed at the prospect of writing a letter. But I did, because like most people, I didn't know how to do it properly at first. I had to learn all the do's and don'ts by trial and error, which was a time-consuming process, though not as formidable as I once imagined it would be.

In the beginning, no one had to persuade me of the importance of correspondence in our lives. By the time I had finished my formal education I already knew how important it would be—personally, socially, and professionally—to write successful letters. I knew that some doors would either open wide or slam shut depending on my composition skills. When you really know something like that, you don't have any choice—you have to master the elements of correspondence. This book is a result of many years of studying everything ever written on the subject, evaluating thousands of letters and memos, and probably writing thousands of them myself.

Some of the other correspondence books that I wrote are largely collections of model letters and memos. This one, too, has plenty of models throughout the text as well as an appendix with models to fit all major categories of correspondence. But unlike the other books, this one is built around the *elements*, or essentials, of correspondence.

Correspondence is surprisingly complex, especially now that we live in a global society and must communicate with people in many different cultures. To add to the complexity, many of us use some form of fast messaging, such as electronic mail (E-mail). E-mail systems and fax machines may have placed additional demands on our skills, but they have also provided a measure of discipline that we all need. It's too expensive, for example, to ramble on and on when you're using E-mail or fax. Also, it's doubtful that E-mail recipients would want to read a ten-page letter on their computer's screen.

Paper mail is still paper mail, and it's increasing every year in spite of some reporters' dreams of a paperless office. Although paper mail may be more familiar to most of us, it doesn't relieve us of responsibility. We have to be literate, and we must know what to say (or not say) and how to say it to produce the results we want.

I'd love to tell you that you can quickly master the elements of correspondence if you just learn about a dozen rules or guidelines. But (are you sitting down?) it's closer to the truth to say that you have to learn about five dozen rules or guidelines. That's the bad news. The good news is that you may have already learned many of the elements in school or at work.

The critical rules and guidelines in correspondence are listed as numbered section titles throughout the book. For example, "26. Be Reasonable," "36. Emphasize the Key Points of Your Message," "47. Avoid Words That Offend," and "49. Use Literal Language." Fifty-nine such sections are arranged in these seven chapters.

1. Introduction to Letter Writing

2. The Importance of Professionalism

3. Getting Ready to Compose a Message

4. Composing the Message

5. Language to Avoid

6. Writing International Messages

7. Mechanics of Correspondence

If you hate to write letters, you may hate it a little less when you finish this book. I won't promise that you'll eagerly wake up early every morning just so you can start writing letters. But often, the more you know about something, the easier it is to do. The easier something is to do, the more likely you'll enjoy doing it.

That's not the main reason, however, that it's important to know the elements of correspondence. Like it or not, we all have to communicate, and good letter-writing skills can enhance your personal, social, and professional lives immeasurably. Don't settle for less.

1

Introduction to Letter Writing

1. Make Correspondence an Asset

The fact that you're reading this book means that you write and send letters and other forms of correspondence. It's something that all literate people do, but how well each person does it is another matter.

Attitude toward Correspondence

If you want to write winning letters, you have to take one step backward before taking one step forward. Before thinking about the essentials of correspondence, such as sentence and paragraph construction, writing style, and message format, stand back and look at yourself. Ask yourself how you feel about writing letters.

Importance of Attitude. The way you feel about correspondence directly affects the way you compose your messages. No matter how much you try to hide it, your attitude shows on paper. If you think of letter writing as a tiresome nuisance or an agonizing chore, it shows just as surely as if you make a face in front of someone after tasting rancid fruit juice. You would be amazed at the ability of many readers to "see" how you feel—on paper.

The Need to Focus on the Positive. If you decide that you should improve your attitude toward this everyday task, concentrate on the positive aspects of letter writing. For everyone who hates to write letters: yes, there are positive aspects. If that weren't the case, people wouldn't be sending millions of personal, social, and business messages every day. The written word would have faded long ago, and communication would be primarily oral. But it isn't. In fact, the number of handwritten, typewritten, and computer-generated messages is increasing dramatically every year, especially if you add expanding global communications to the total.

Correspondence as an Asset

Whether correspondence is an asset or a liability is up to you. You have to decide if you want to make it an asset and then take the necessary steps to realize that objective.

How Correspondence Can Be an Asset. Think about some of the ways in which correspondence can be an asset.

- It can help you save the time, effort, and expense of a face-to-face business meeting or personal visit.
- It can help you promote goodwill for you and your employer.
- It can create and solidify personal and business relationships.
- It can help you handle routine personal and business matters quickly and efficiently.
- It can provide a written record for your files.
- It can help you promote ideas, products, and services.
- It can help you reach people virtually anywhere, even in remote parts of the world.
- It can help you enrich your life through the exchange of information and friendship with others.
- It can help you secure a better job or a promotion.
- It can help you motivate others to respond or act as you would like them to do.
- It can help you express yourself more carefully and clearly than you might be able to do in person.
- It can help you create the image you want to project to others.
- It can help you prevent or correct misunderstandings and problems.

How to Make a Letter an Asset. To make letter writing an asset instead of a liability, you have to distinguish between a mere letter and a *successful* letter. An unsuccessful letter fails to do what it should do, even if the objective is simply to make someone feel good or to convey certain information clearly. A successful letter is an asset rather than a liability.

Assume that you want to write a brief message of congratulations on a friend's job promotion. This shouldn't be an overwhelming task, should it? The two of you are good friends and have spent many hours talking and joking with each other. So all you have to do is be yourself, right? Not necessarily. For example, which of the following letters is best—the one that adds a typically (for you) humorous, conversational tone or the one that is more straightforward?

Dear Jim,

Congratulations! That's a nice little job you landed. But then, some people have all the luck!

Hope you make a mint in your new position. If anyone can do it, you can.

All the best.

Regards,

Dear Jim,

Congratulations on your promotion! It's a great opportunity, Jim, and I can't think of anyone who deserves it more.

Your company is really lucky to have you at the helm of its engineering division. I know you'll enjoy the challenge, and I hope you'll have many exciting and rewarding days ahead in your new post.

Best regards,

If you picked the straightforward version (the second one), you were right. Even with a close friend who is used to your good-natured kidding, humor is risky in this situation. It detracts from the reader's moment of glory, and if the message is read the wrong way or at the wrong time (and you can't control how or when someone reads a letter), it could sound like a touch of envy. Although that may be the furthest thing from your mind, if it happens, the letter has become a liability. It not only has failed to achieve what you want to accomplish—compliment your friend and express genuine, unqualified happiness for him—but, additionally, may have created an unfavorable image of you as someone harboring inner resentment at your friend's good fortune.

You can see, then, how easily—and unintentionally—a letter can become a liability. Avoiding that mistake and making a letter an asset takes thought, planning, and serious attention to the smallest details.

2. Create Effective Messages

It is widely accepted among writing authorities that effective messages will enhance your career and improve your personal and social relationships. So if your letters are bland and ineffective, or if they appear more or less adequate but not outstanding, you're probably just going through the motions—stringing words together as hastily and painlessly as possible. Much more is needed to create truly effective letters that produce significant rewards.

Categories of Correspondence

It would be helpful if a single set of rules existed for all types of messages. But different rules apply to different types of letters. A business sales letter, for example, has far different requirements than a personal birthday greeting has; a goodwill social letter involves a different tone than a business letter of complaint involves; and a letter of commendation provokes a very different response than a letter of dismissal provokes.

Letters You May Write. Think of the many different types of letters you may write in your lifetime.

Acknowledgments	Inquiries
Adjustments	Instructions
Announcements	Introductions
Apologies	Invitations
Appointments	Orders
Appreciation	Personnel
Collections	Proposals
Complaints	Recommendations
Congratulations	References
Credit	Reminders
Explanations	Requests
Follow-ups	Sales
Goodwill	Sympathy
Holiday wishes	Thanks

Regardless of the category, however, certain qualities are common in nearly every effective message, as described in the next section. For examples of letters in these categories, refer to the appendix.

Characteristics of Effective Messages

One type of letter may differ from another in length, tone, writing style, degree of formality, format, and other matters. Nevertheless, certain general qualities will increase the effectiveness of most messages.

- *The way you say something is as important as what you say.* For example, a cold, indifferent, unfriendly, critical, or antagonistic tone ("Let me make one thing perfectly clear") will put a reader on the defensive and is likely to encourage a negative response. See Sections 22, 26, 27, and 29 in Chapter 4 and Section 47 in Chapter 5.

- *Simple, clear writing contributes to better reader comprehension and prevents costly misunderstandings.* Long, complex, abstract words, and rambling, cumbersome sentences and paragraphs won't impress anyone. ("In support of the recommendation to compartmentalize the unit and expedite interdepartmental processing of substantive extracontractual requests, I am hereby entering into circulation the following policy directive.") They'll make you appear muddled and incoherent and may cause misinterpretation and unwanted responses from readers. See Section 32 in Chapter 4, Section 42 in Chapter 5, and Section 51 in Chapter 6.
- *A natural, friendly writing style encourages a favorable response from readers.* Although foreign readers frown on too much familiarity and informality, domestic readers respond more favorably to a conversational writing style. ("I was delighted to receive an early copy of your new report. It's wonderful!") In the United States, a formal style is considered unfriendly and uninviting and often sounds phony. ("Please accept my gratitude for the advance copy of your new report. Let me compliment you on your esteemed achievement.") See Sections 22, 24, 27, and 29 in Chapter 4.
- *Accuracy is essential in all correspondence.* Although readers know that everyone makes mistakes, they are very unforgiving of those who make informational, grammatical, stylistic, or other errors in letters. See Chapter 2.
- *A letter that gets to the point without delay creates a good impression.* Readers are annoyed when they have to read several paragraphs before finding out the purpose of a letter. See Section 35 in Chapter 4.
- *A letter should have a clear, concise conclusion.* Avoid rambling conclusions or endings that appear to introduce new topics or resume the previous topic. If you're asking readers to do something, give one clear suggestion.

("Mail this form with your payment of $16.98 today.")
See Section 40 in Chapter 4.

- *Archaic words, expressions, and letter elements will make you appear out of touch and uninformed.* Although trendy expressions (*homeboy*), business jargon (*downsize*), and relatively new expressions (*user friendly*) should be avoided in all general correspondence, particularly with a foreign audience, archaic expressions and elements are just as bad. Use contemporary elements, such as *Dear* rather than *My dear* for salutations. Also, eliminate archaic terminology, such as *thanking you in advance* and *duly noted*, from the body of the letter. See Section 43 in Chapter 5.

- *Readers like to be addressed personally in a letter.* It makes a reader feel good to see his or her name mentioned in the body of a letter. Frequent use of the word "you" has a similar effect in domestic writing. ("Would *you* be interested in . . . ?") The opposite may be true in foreign correspondence, however. In Japan, for example, business readers prefer that you emphasize their companies rather than the individual. ("Would *your company* be interested in . . . ?") See Section 22 in Chapter 4.

- *A consistent writing style appears professional and is less likely to confuse or annoy a reader.* Capitalize and spell terms consistently throughout your letters, and use a consistent style of punctuation. Readers are disturbed by sudden shifts in spelling, hyphenation, and capitalization from sentence to sentence or paragraph to paragraph. They are similarly confused by shifts from heavy to light punctuation. See Sections 11, 12, and 13 in Chapter 2.

- *The active voice is more effective than the passive voice in correspondence.* The active voice (*he said*) is much more forceful and concise than the passive voice (*it was said*). The passive voice is preferred, however, when you don't want to be direct or explicit, such as when you want to explain something without mentioning or criticizing a particular person. See Section 33 in Chapter 4.

- *Some words can be provocative or sound negative in a certain context.* Eliminate words that might wound the reader if used in a critical or accusative context. ("You *claim* that your check was lost." "Your work is *unacceptable*.") See Section 47 in Chapter 5.
- *A letter must always be tailored to the audience.* Study your readers before you compose your message. Age, social environment, religious customs, political views, level of education, and other reader characteristics should be considered in choosing terminology, in deciding how much detail to provide, and in determining the degree of formality to use. See Section 21 in Chapter 4.
- *Pet phrases are annoying to readers.* Letter writers usually don't realize that they are overusing certain pet phrases (*for the record, as you know, the bottom line is*). Many of these phrases are unnecessary and contribute nothing to the meaning of a letter. If repeated in a letter, they can be especially annoying to readers. See Sections 45 and 46 in Chapter 5.
- *Wordiness and repetition usually impede the reader.* Look for unnecessary words in your letters (*in the year of* 1993; *in view of the fact that* [because]; first *and foremost*). But don't eliminate words that contribute to smooth sentence and paragraph transition and the logical flow of your thoughts (*however; therefore*), and don't eliminate additional words or sentences or intentional repetition that will help a foreign reader better understand your message. See Sections 37 and 38 in Chapter 4.
- *Organization and planning are as important in correspondence as they are in larger documents.* Unless you are a skilled writer, it may help you present your thoughts in a clear, orderly manner if you first jot down what you want to accomplish and then briefly list and organize the key points you want to make in your letter. See Chapter 3.
- *Difficult letters are best written when you are alert and refreshed.* It's always a mistake to write difficult letters,

such as a letter of complaint or an important proposal, when you're tired. Fatigue and errors go hand in hand, and irritability and impatience with others are much more likely to surface when you're tired. See Section 26 in Chapter 4.

- *The mechanics of correspondence can have as much impact on a reader as what you say will have.* The format you use—the layout of the various letter elements on the page—gives readers their first impression of you before they read the details of your message. (For more about format, refer to Section 5.) Even a brilliant message may be lost if you use an ugly layout and have a page full of messy corrections. See Chapter 7.

- *Professional writing won't disguise bad advice.* Whereas good advice is often lost in a poorly composed letter, bad advice is rarely camouflaged by correct composition. Eventually, the reader will realize that the advice is inferior to the composition that presents it.

3. BUILD A FAVORABLE IMAGE WITH YOUR LETTERS

One of the most important objectives of letter writing is to build a favorable image. If you're writing a personal or social letter, you want to present yourself in the best possible light. If you're writing a business letter, you want to enhance not only your own image but your company's image as well. Since a reader forms a first impression just by looking at a letter, you have to be concerned about the physical appearance of your correspondence as well as what you say and how you say it.

Although it may not be fair, readers will equate weaknesses in your letters with weaknesses in you or your company. For example:

- If your letter has typographical errors, your readers may conclude that you probably make errors in your facts as well.

- If your writing style is stiff and formal, they may think that you're out of touch with contemporary life or that you're a cold person who will be difficult to deal with.

- If you use a lot of big, complex words and sentences unnecessarily, they may decide that you're pretentious and snobbish.

- If you use negative or antagonistic words, they may think that you're argumentive and hard to get along with.

None of these impressions may be correct, but if readers don't know you personally, they have only your correspondence to guide them in making a judgment.

What Your Messages Reveal

Letters, memos, and other messages reveal more about you than you might expect. They may not tell a reader whether you are tall or short or have brown eyes or blue eyes, but they will reveal a lot about your character.

By reading your correspondence, readers will form opinions about you, such as whether you're professional or unprofessional, considerate or inconsiderate, sincere or insincere, natural or affected, cooperative or uncooperative, industrious or lazy, informed or uninformed, careful or careless, concerned or indifferent, and intelligent or unintelligent. Although these impressions are not always accurate, they can be manipulated through writing style.

Letter writers, in fact, often do not portray themselves accurately on paper. Some people intentionally create an impressive image that they don't live up to in person. Other people have a serious block about letter writing and, as a result, create an unfavorable image that doesn't do them justice. Most of the time, people who present an image that's worse than they really are don't even realize that they're hurting themselves unnecessarily.

An Image-Building Program

Successful letter writers work hard to be objective and self-analytical. They take time to examine their correspondence and "listen" to the way they sound on paper. It takes a sharp eye and ear for someone to read his or her own correspondence and see the same portrait that a reader will visualize.

Steps to Take. If you want to improve the image that you reflect in your correspondence, try following four simple steps.

1. *Decide what image you want to project.* How would you like to have the reader visualize you or your company? Write a brief one- or two-sentence summary of the "perfect" (for you) image. Or develop a list of the essential qualities, such as professionalism and sincerity, that you want readers to think you have. For example, "I want my readers to think that I am bright, honest, trustworthy, conscientious, loyal, concerned about their welfare, helpful, hardworking, accurate, and professional."

2. *Always reread your correspondence—more than once if necessary—before sending it.* If time will allow, set your message aside and return to it later with a fresh outlook.

3. *Become a ruthless critic of your own work.* Make a checklist of questions, such as the following, to ask yourself.

   ( ) Does my letter look neat and clean?
   ( ) Is it properly formatted?
   ( ) Does it have an effective opening and closing?
   ( ) Have I used short, simple words, sentences, and paragraphs?

( ) Have I used positive language?
( ) Have I adopted a courteous, friendly, sincere tone?
( ) Is the terminology appropriate for my reader?
( ) Have I used contemporary language and letter
    elements?
( ) Are the key points presented in a clear, logical order?
( ) Have I rechecked my facts to be certain they are accurate
    and up to date?

Review the table of contents and index in this book for ideas about other questions you might want to add to this list.

4. *Look again at your perfect-image summary or list (Step 1) and search for ways in which your letter fails to reflect that image.* Then revise the letter as much as necessary to correct the weaknesses that will project an unfavorable image of you or your company.

The usual response to this four-step image-building program for correspondence is: I don't have time to do all that. Many successful letter writers once said the same thing. But as they watched the rewards of successful image building linger out of reach, they decided that they would have to make the time.

Like most repetitive acts, the four suggested steps should soon become a habit that can be handled in seconds rather than minutes. However, since a favorable personal or company image can bring you or your company increased benefits, the investment of even a few extra minutes on a message will in time pay for itself.

4. USE YOUR LETTERS TO CREATE BONDS

People need people both personally and professionally. Not everyone, however, is thrilled about having to depend on others. To them, developing and maintaining a personal or professional relationship is a necessary evil. But most people enjoy human interaction and welcome opportunities to create better relations with family, friends, neighbors, coworkers, and customers or clients.

The Letter as a Bonding Agent

You will not likely find another bonding agent as effective, inexpensive, and readily available to everyone as a letter or any other type of handwritten, typed, printed, or electronically prepared message. Why?

- A message can be prepared by anyone who can read or write.
- A letter is relatively inexpensive to prepare and send (compared to the time and cost of a personal visit, for example).
- People love to receive letters and tend to respond positively to a well-written message and favorably toward the writer of an effective message.

Using Your Letters to Create Bonds

Taking the Initiative. If you want to use your letters to create bonds with others, you have to work at it. Sending a letter routinely without evidence of personal interest or involvement isn't enough. The same would be true if you met someone in person and wanted to develop a personal or professional bond. Merely saying hello and commenting on the weather wouldn't be enough to develop even a weak relationship. You would have to smile warmly, initiate or actively participate in conversation, compliment the person or in some other way make the person feel good, make an effort to discuss or do things of interest to the person, offer your help if assistance is needed, and generally take deliberate steps to open the door to future communication or shared activity. You must do the same in your correspondence.

Considering the Other Person. If you seriously want to create or strengthen a bond with someone, you need to evaluate both the situation or environment in which this relationship will be formed and the character and needs of the other person. First, do you want to develop a strong relationship with a client or customer? With someone in your community or neighborhood? With a member of your family? Next, what do you know about this person? What type of relationship would this person be receptive to? To which of the person's interests or needs could you contribute something useful? How could you enrich this person's business or personal life? Finally, are you prepared to make the relationship as beneficial to the other person as it will be to you?

Some letter writers fail to create effective bonds because they only evaluate their own environment and their own needs. They may, for example, want to enhance their social standing in the community or increase sales at work. Sometimes they become so preoccupied with what they want from someone else that they forget the other person's needs. Forging a bond requires a reciprocal relationship, which means that it's essential to give in order to receive. Once that proposition becomes clear, a major obstacle to successful bonding will be overcome.

Making Helpful Comments. Here are some examples of things you can say in your letters to create or strengthen the bonds in your personal and professional life. Notice that a major objective is to encourage the other person to think that you are someone he or she would like to know better.

- Use every possible occasion to make contact with the other person: "We appreciate having you as a customer and send you our sincerest wishes for a peaceful and bountiful New Year."
- Make the reader feel good by saying something nice: "As always, Jill, I appreciated your meticulous evaluation."

- Mention the person's name one or more times in the letter: "We appreciate your interest, Mr. Weiland."
- Adopt the "you" approach in your domestic correspondence: "As a resident of Green Palms like you, I know how much you value your privacy."
- Use friendly, pleasing language: "Thanks to your prompt and thoughtful reply, Jean, I was able to complete the project on schedule."
- Invite further communication by asking a question: "May we discuss your copying problems with you?"
- Apologize sincerely when you're wrong, and even if you're not wrong, express concern if someone is unhappy: "I am so sorry that our new policy has caused a problem for you."
- Take the first step in issuing invitations: "I've asked some colleagues to come for cocktails on Friday, May 6, at five o'clock. Will you join us?"
- Send something of interest to the reader: "I thought you might like to see the enclosed article on bass fishing."
- Make your statements positive or uplifting: "Now that our plant has been rebuilt following the hurricane last year, we are eager to get down to the pleasant business of serving loyal customers such as you."
- Be genuinely sympathetic if someone has suffered a loss: "I was so sorry to hear about the fire that destroyed your beautiful home. I know how much it meant to you."
- Be a willing and cooperative friend and respond enthusiastically to requests for help: "Count me in, Jim. I'd be delighted to help you set up the display next Friday."

All of these examples have one thing in common—a warm, sincere tone with a direct focus on the other person and his or her needs and interests. You'll find that those two ingredients will act like a magnet in drawing people toward you and in strengthening the bonds you create through your letters.

5. CHOOSE THE RIGHT STYLE AND FORMAT FOR YOUR MESSAGES

Both format and style affect the appearance of a letter. *Format* refers to a letter's physical layout and arrangement of elements on the page. *Style* refers to the distinctive treatment of words, such as the capitalization, punctuation, and spelling of elements and other words in a letter.

First Impressions

Importance of First Impressions. When you receive a letter, you probably glance at it before you begin reading, just as you would look at a person before you begin talking. Although it may seem illogical to suggest that the appearance of a letter has a greater impact than its content, the way it looks is more important in one respect. People tend to form first impressions of everything they see and stubbornly cling to those original images. If the appearance of your letter doesn't appeal to a reader, that initial impression may adversely affect the reader's response to your message.

The Appearance of a Letter. If you open a letter and, before reading it, notice that the type looks faded, you may wonder if the letter comes from someone who isn't doing well enough financially to buy a new ribbon or who is just too lazy and unprofessional to change it. If you see smudges on the letter, you may visualize an unkempt person with dirty hands. If you see tiny margins and strange spacing between the elements of the letter, you may wonder if the writer is uneducated or if the person works in a business where letter writing is such a rare occurrence that the writer never learned how to do it correctly. In all of these cases, you formed an unfavorable first impression of the writer from the appearance of his or her letter.

Format

Think of your letter as a photograph or watercolor painting to be matted and framed. You want to have the mat be the right size and to have the photograph or painting centered properly and attractively within the frame. Your letters deserve as much attention. They, too, need the correct margins (mat) and should be centered properly and attractively within the page (frame).

Formatting Tips. A basic formula in letter formatting is that the more white space your letter has, the better it will look. Some letter writers try to crowd everything they have to say on one page, using tiny left and right margins, with the type squashed tight against the letterhead address at the top of the page and nearly running off the page at the bottom. Such an unattractive, crowded layout creates a poor impression.

In the past, busy letter writers who used typewriters were disinclined to retype an entire letter from scratch just to position it more attractively on the page. Now, however, with the use of computers, there is no excuse for sending out an improperly formatted letter. All the writer needs to do is type in different format specifications, and the computer will automatically readjust the letter. Many computer programs even have a print-preview feature that enables the writer to see a letter's appearance before it is printed out.

A properly formatted letter is well balanced and looks pleasing. It makes the content clear and easy to read. Since a chief objective of every letter should be to help readers digest the content and avoid misreading, a clean, neat, open format is desired to enhance, not detract from, the message itself. To keep the letter as neat and simple as possible, computer users should resist the temptation to use different typefaces or other graphics within a letter and leave such flairs and flourishes to bulletins, newsletters, and magazines.

Principal Formats. The five standard letter formats are the full-block, block, modified-block, simplified, and personal formats. Chapter 7 illustrates each letter format (Section 55), including examples of proper envelope formats (Section 58.)

The standard formats are appropriate for business, social, and personal stationery that has a printed letterhead. Social and personal letters written on plain paper without a printed return address can generally be formatted the same as a business letter, although the writer's return address must then be added at the very top of the page. (The return address is often omitted in letters to family members and very close friends.) Refer to Section 54 in Chapter 7 for a discussion of stationery.

Chapter 7 also illustrates a standard memo format (Section 55) used in interoffice correspondence and in some forms of fast messaging, such as electronic mail, and standard formal-correspondence formats (Section 59).

Format Elements. Many of the principal elements of letters and memos, such as the date and signature, are positioned differently on the page, depending on the format being used. Each of the following key letter elements are described in Section 56 of Chapter 7: date, reference line, personal or confidential notation, inside address, attention line, salutation, subject line, body, complimentary close, signature, identification line, enclosure notation, mail notation, copy notation, postscript, and continuation-page heading.

The following key memo elements are also described in Section 56: guide headings (*To, From, Date, Reference, Subject*), body, identification line, enclosure notation, mail notation, copy notation, postscript, and continuation-page heading. Refer to Section 57 in Chapter 7 for a description of the correct personal and professional titles, such as *Ms., Mrs., Mr.,* and *Dr.,* to use in the inside address and salutation.

Style

Personal and business letter writers should be concerned about three things regarding style (capitalization, punctuation, and spelling).

- *Is the style consistent throughout your letter?* If you don't capitalize, punctuate, and spell consistently, it may confuse or annoy the reader and will give the impression that you're careless and unprofessional.
- *Is the style up to date?* No one wants to appear old-fashioned and behind the times.
- *Is the style appropriate for your reader?* It may be necessary to use different styles for different readers. In domestic correspondence, for example, the trend is to use less punctuation; in foreign correspondence, it is essential to use more punctuation to guide a reader unfamiliar with English through each sentence.

The style you use will tell your readers a lot about your professionalism—or lack of it. In fact, this subject is such an important aspect of correspondence that the entire next chapter is devoted to it.

6. KNOW WHEN A HANDWRITTEN LETTER IS APPROPRIATE

Some people prepare all of their correspondence by typewriter or computer. Others write all personal and social correspondence by hand and even send a lot of handwritten notes at work. Still others prepare social and business correspondence by typewriter or computer but write all personal letters to family and friends by hand.

Changing Rules

Handwritten Messages. The rules about what should or should not be handwritten are much less strict today than they were two or more decades ago. At one time, it was considered rude and ignorant to type a personal letter or to use

handwriting for a business letter. Most authorities now realize that it is foolish to ask people whose handwriting is barely
legible to write every personal letter by hand. They also agree
that it is equally foolish to expect harried businesspeople to
take time to type every brief one- or two-sentence note to
coworkers and close business associates. The consensus
today, then, is that you may do as you wish with most business notes, such as this one to a coworker.

From the Desk of

DONNA WINSLOW-CHARTIER

*Tim, here's the material you requested. Call if you have
any questions.*

Best, Donna

For such a brief message, many businesspeople would use
a small note-style memo (*From the desk of . . .*) or a self-
sticking commercial note. It simply doesn't warrant the use of
official business letterhead stationery and the transcription
time a secretary would need to prepare it. Common sense,
therefore, is a determining factor nowadays in deciding
whether to use handwriting or typewriter/computer preparation.

Typewritten and Computer Messages. Common sense
should also apply when a very different situation is involved.
For example, if you are thanking a prominent person in the
community for speaking at your social organization's ban-
quet or a prominent businessperson for speaking at your
company's seminar, you should send a properly formatted,
typed or computer-prepared letter on standard business letterhead. If you are acknowledging a customer's order, you
should also use a standard business letter or an appropriate
reply form. Usually, any such correspondence going to an

outside party in which you are writing on behalf of a social or business organization should be typed or prepared by computer.

Formal Correspondence

Formal invitations, announcements, and similar types of formal correspondence are printed or engraved. Semiformal invitations, such as an invitation to a Thanksgiving party at your home, may be handwritten on small-size personal stationery or a foldover card or sheet. Also, stationery stores sell fill-in cards for such occasions. Replies to formal or semiformal correspondence are always handwritten in the same formal or semiformal style as the invitation, unless a formal check-off reply card is enclosed for your use. Refer to Section 59 in Chapter 7 for the proper style and format to use in formal correspondence.

Occasions That Require Personal Emphasis

When a Personal Touch Is Needed. If you want a short note to be more personal and intimate, use handwriting. Certain occasions call for a personal touch, such as the death of a friend or associate, the receipt of a gift from a friend or relative, or a note of congratulations from a friend or neighbor. It would be offensive and cold, in fact, to type such a note, when the occasion clearly requires a warm and very personal message.

Examples of Personal Messages. The following messages are examples of those that should be handwritten on small personal stationery or foldover cards or sheets. If you use a printed commercial card, such as a birthday or anniversary card, be certain to pen your own message on the card in black or other dark ink.

Dear Aunt Helen,

I don't know how to thank you for the magnificent book on China. What a beauty! I can hardly wait to start reading.

You couldn't have picked a better gift for someone who loves the Far East as much as I do. A million thanks, Aunt Helen.

Love,

Dear Ed,

Madge and I want to send you our deepest sympathy on the death of Shari. I know that she will be greatly missed by everyone who knew her, and we all share your grief during this very difficult time.

Please let us know, Ed, if there's anything we can do to help.

With sincere sympathy,

Dear Marilyn,

How wonderful that you and John will be celebrating your twentieth wedding anniversary on Sunday! All of us in the department hope you have a beautiful day together.

Congratulations to both of you, and may you have many more years of happiness.

Very best wishes,

How to Decide whether a Message Should Be Handwritten. If you still have doubts about which messages should be handwritten, ask yourself whether the message is a reply to formal correspondence, such as a wedding invitation; whether it will be short, such as one to four sentences; whether it contains a personal, rather than a company or business, message; and whether the occasion prompting the message involves emotional circumstances, such as a celebration or a death. Such messages should usually be handwritten by pen (not pencil).

7. USE FORM LETTERS TO SAVE TIME

Purpose of Form Letters

Form letters—standard messages used over and over—represent a special category of business correspondence. They were originally created to save time when the same message was often sent to different people.

Formerly, the practice was to type a standard message and have a supply printed on company letterhead. Sometimes a typist would later type in the date, inside address, salutation, and certain facts or figures that might differ from one letter to another.

Eventually, automated typewriters and then computers were used to merge the standard message with the data that varied from letter to letter. Then and now, however, the purpose of using form letters has been to avoid having to compose and retype similar letters from scratch each time.

Although vast quantities of a standard message can be printed, the computer makes it possible to store a standard message and recall it later for editing and printout. You can also store stock sentences and paragraphs in the computer and copy them into different individual letters.

Preparing Form Letters

Style and Format. You should prepare a form letter in the same format as that used for your other business letters. (Refer to the sample form letter in Section 55 of Chapter 7.) Your punctuation, capitalization, and spelling style should also be the same. But other things differ. You cannot, for example, tailor the message to a particular individual; rather, you have to slant it toward a group or class of people who all will be receiving the same message. But you can still make the message appear personal by typing in specific names and other facts or having such data merged by your computer with the standard message.

Form-Letter Effectiveness

Effectiveness Checklist. Since form letters and stock sentences and paragraphs have special requirements beyond those of individual letters, you need a different set of rules to evaluate their effectiveness. For example:

- Study the letters in your files to determine whether it would be practical to replace certain individual letters with form letters in the future.
- Design the form letters so that computer merges or typed fill-ins can be made easily.
- Be certain that your message will be easily understood on the first reading.
- Avoid old-fashioned language, such as "reference is made to" and "you are hereby advised that."
- Be certain that your message involves a routine business or informational matter pertinent to many people.
- Format your letter so that the address will show in a window envelope.
- Identify each letter, such as by placing a number in one of the corners.

- Use a systematic numbering system for the various form letters and subsequent revisions.
- Ask yourself, if you were receiving the message, would you consider it effective and attractive?
- Prepare a set of standards that all form letters must meet.
- Prepare written instructions that explain when a form letter may be used, how many copies should be made, and which enclosures (if any) should be included.

Other Factors Affecting Form-Letter Effectiveness. Although your form-letter system may be perfect in every way, a letter's effectiveness can still be diminished by low-quality printing, a signature that is obviously rubber-stamped (or omitted completely), and other carelessness in appearance or accuracy. In such matters, the same guidelines described in this book that apply to individual messages also apply to standard messages.

8. PREPARE TO SEND AND RECEIVE ELECTRONIC MESSAGES

How Electronic Mail Works

Electronic mail (E-mail) is a form of computerized message transmission. Users can be connected to one another by computer within a company or within a network outside the company. By subscribing to an E-mail network service, a member, using a password or access code, can transmit messages to any other member anywhere on the E-mail network. The connection is made by using a modem and a telephone. The modem converts a computer-prepared message into signals that will travel over the telephone lines to a specified destination, where the signals are converted back into computer-readable form.

Since a user might send a message at any time of the day or night, even when the recipient isn't there to receive it, the message is stored in computer memory (called an electronic "mailbox") at the destination, waiting for the recipient. After turning on the computer and discovering that a message is waiting, the recipient can bring up the message on his or her computer screen for immediate reading or print it out in hard-copy form.

Fast Messaging

Advantages of Fast-Messaging Systems. The appeal of E-mail and other forms of fast messaging is speed. Depending on the length of a message, it can be transmitted in mere seconds or minutes, unlike traditional postal or private-delivery mail, which takes one or more days to be delivered. The same message can also be programmed to go to numerous recipients, without preparing individual copies as you would have to do to distribute paper mail.

E-mail resembles telex transmission, an older form of fast messaging, in its speed and the use of telephone lines to send messages. Facsimile (fax) machines also use the telephone lines to transmit messages. An independent fax machine (not connected to a computer) can be used only for transmission, however, not message preparation. With E-mail, a message is both prepared on and sent by one computer to another computer that also can both prepare and send messages.

E-Mail Requirements

Preparation. Most of the guidelines in this book applying to traditional correspondence also apply to E-mail. Although E-mail programs require the use of certain access and transmission codes, and senders commonly use more abbreviations, such as *BTW,* "by the way," you should use the same general punctuation, capitalization, and spelling style that you use for your paper mail. But there are two notable exceptions to traditional correspondence in E-mail preparation.

- It is more practical, though not mandatory, to prepare E-mail messages in a memo format, rather than in a letter format, using standard guide-word headings.

```
DATE:    January 5, 1995
TO:      Aileen Carpenter-Bose
FROM:    Jason Autasheare Jr.
SUBJECT: Fall Seminar
```

Section 55 in Chapter 7 has an illustration of a complete message prepared in one of the common memo formats.
- E-mail messages of no more than one standard page are the most effective and the least expensive. A longer message takes longer to transmit and thus costs more. Also, recipients who want to read their incoming messages on a computer screen, rather than print out a hard copy, often find lengthy messages difficult to follow. If you want to be certain that an E-mail message will be read completely, keep it short.

E-Mail Problems

Disadvantages of E-Mail. E-mail has some disadvantages that traditional paper mail doesn't have.

- If adequate security doesn't exist on your system or the recipient's system, other users on the E-mail network can retrieve and read the messages you send or receive. In E-mail terminology, a message is then posted on a public "bulletin board" (BBS) for everyone to read.

- For other users on your network to know that you have sent them a message, they have to turn on their computers. If they don't, your message has to wait. So before you send anything urgent by E-mail, be certain that the recipients normally have their computers turned on.
- You won't necessarily escape junk mail or other nonessential messages by using an E-mail network. The speed and ease with which an E-mail message can be sent tend to encourage, not discourage, nonessential chit-chat.
- If you send messages that recipients should print out and file in hard-copy form and that you, too, need to print out and file, a major advantage of E-mail is lost. (Some recipients simply won't go to the trouble of printing a paper copy even if you want them to do so.) You may as well just distribute paper copies to everyone in the beginning.
- E-mail, because of its speed and because computer enthusiasts love it, is often used, or misused, for messages that should be conveyed face to face, through a personal telephone call, or in a personal handwritten message. It would be inappropriate, for example, to send a message of sympathy, a congratulatory message, or a thank you note by E-mail. Certain messages require a warmer, more human touch than the cold, technical approach that electronic messaging portrays to many people.

In spite of the increasing popularity of all forms of fast messaging, users of E-mail and other advanced systems need to evaluate their usage regularly and learn to recognize when traditional paper correspondence is more secure, confidential, personal, human, and effective.

2

The Importance of Professionalism

9. USE LANGUAGE TO ENHANCE YOUR PROFESSIONALISM

The Pursuit of Professionalism

Professionalism is a common topic in many business and social circles. When you consider the popularity of self-improvement programs, it becomes obvious why professionalism is one of the most sought-after attributes in the modern world. It's widely considered a necessary component of success, and the letters you write will readily reveal to others whether or not you have it.

Definition of a Professional. Broadly, the word *professional* is used to describe not only someone who engages in a particular type of work, such as a lawyer, but also anyone who behaves and performs properly, successfully, and according to high standards in all aspects of life. In fact, a person's standing at work and in the community depends in part on the degree of professionalism he or she achieves.

Strategies for Professionalism. People use many different strategies to increase their professional attributes and to project an aura of professionalism. They may go to school, expand their reading and other independent study, or join business and social clubs. Since most people live and work in an environment in which they need to communicate with others, professionals also must try to improve their language skills.

Language as a Tool

Can you think of a more useful tool to increase the professional appearance of your letters than the language you use? Most people, however, have taken for granted their correspondence and the language they use in it. Unfortunately, that type of inattention can create a serious problem. When we don't pay proper attention to something, we tend to become careless and misuse it. We also tend to overlook potential benefits and miss potentially rewarding opportunities. In view of the importance of language to everyday life in any organized society, it deserves our full respect.

Using Language Advantageously. Your correspondence offers ongoing opportunities to make language work for you—at home, in the community, and in business. It's a perfect arena for exercises in professionalism. For example, by using the language in your letters advantageously, you can:

- Win arguments with persuasive language: "If this measure is approved, the proposed changes will be especially beneficial to you and your family."
- Forge important relationships with tactful language: "I'm very eager to help you establish new sales records and would like to begin with these two suggestions."
- Elicit confidence from others with clear, logical language: "I would appreciate it if you would review my accomplishments during the past two years. These four contributions, for example, have increased word processing output in our department by 35 percent."
- Stimulate a positive attitude toward you with pleasing, friendly language: "I wish you could be here with us today."

The objective is to decide what you want to accomplish and tailor the language in your messages to that goal. This task isn't as simple as it may seem, however. Whenever you adapt language to a particular situation, you need to deal with numerous factors, from word choice to tone, and you need to be certain that you're using correct grammar and an effective punctuation and capitalization style. The next sections in this chapter, as well as those in Chapters 3 through 6, discuss all of these concerns.

10. USE GOOD GRAMMAR IN YOUR MESSAGES

Nothing torpedoes an attempt to write a professional message faster than incorrect grammar. Unless the recipient's grasp of grammar is equally weak, any mistakes you make may as well be highlighted in large bold type. Contrary to popular opinion, it's usually wishful thinking to assume that no one will notice. Grammatical errors, in fact, rarely escape the attention of an educated, professional reader.

Evaluating Your Grammar

Reread copies of letters you sent in the past year or two and focus on the grammatical composition. Even if you can't find any errors, if you suspect that your grammar may be less than perfect, it probably is. The fact that you're uneasy and have some doubts, however, may be good. If you thought your grammar was perfect but it wasn't, you wouldn't know anything was wrong and therefore wouldn't be motivated to examine it and try to improve it.

When rereading copies of your correspondence, don't be dismayed if you discover some errors. Even competent letter writers make occasional errors in grammar. Sometimes such mistakes are a result of carelessness. Perhaps the letter writer was in too much of a hurry. Or perhaps the writer had developed a bad habit of sending letters without carefully proofreading them. Notice the obvious verb error in the first paragraph; it was probably made in haste rather than in ignorance.

Dear Sally,

We were so happy to get your card from
London and hope you enjoyed England as much
as we did last year. No, we *have* never *seen* the
Concorde, but our oldest son, Tim, *seen* [*has seen*]
it many times.

When you have a moment, we'd love to hear
more about your travels.

Hope you're both well. Everyone is fine over
here--and busy!

Love,

Correcting Your Grammar

If the errors were caused by carelessness and you really know
better, you should be able to spot them as you reread copies
of your letters. In the future, then, you can avoid this type of
error simply by taking time to proofread and correct all of
your messages before sending them out.

What about the grammatical rules you may be breaking
without knowing it? In this case, you won't know what to
look for, so it may be beneficial to review the latest edition of
a grammar book, such as *The Elements of Grammar*
(Macmillan). After refreshing your memory, once again examine file copies of your correspondence. This time it should be
easier to spot the mistakes you previously missed.

Common Grammatical Errors. Some grammatical mistakes
in letters are more common than others, and you should be
especially watchful for such errors, because they are the most
likely to find their way into your messages. For example:

- A verb must agree with the subject of the sentence in
  number: "The *association* of accountants *is* [not *are*]

meeting today." Some writers may mistakenly assume that the plural word *accountants* is the subject of the sentence, but it's the object of the preposition *of*; the word *association* is the subject.

- Words that imply "the most that there can be" should not be compared: "He has the *perfect* [not *most perfect* or *more perfect*] solution." Something that is perfect is already the most that it can be, so it cannot be *more* or *most* perfect.

- Most masculine forms of nouns are now used for both masculine and feminine references: "The *director* [not *directress*] of the research center resigned last week." In some cases, an entirely new word, such as *salesperson*, has been coined to avoid the need to use separate terms, such as *salesman* and *saleswoman*. "A *businessperson* [not *businessman* or *businesswoman*] must strive to be professional at all times."

- The proper tense of a verb must be used to express time accurately: "By the time you receive this letter, I *will have finished* [not *will finish*] the report." Since the report will be completed before a specific time in the future when the recipient will get the letter, the future *perfect* tense is required, not the future tense.

- An adverb, not an adjective, must be used to modify a verb: "She types *slowly* [not *slow*] when the material is highly technical." *Slowly* describes "how" she types (verb); hence the adverb form *slowly* is required. *Slow* is an adjective, and adjectives modify nouns, not verbs. "My clock is *slow*." *Slow* modifies the noun *clock*.

The preceding examples are only a few of the hundreds of common grammatical mistakes that letter writers make. But an error is an error. Whether or not it is a *common* error, it will detract from the professional appearance of your letter and your professionalism as an individual.

11. DEVELOP A CLEAR PUNCTUATION STYLE

If you're wondering what punctuation has to do with professionalism, the answer is, "A lot." Too much or too little punctuation can make a letter a nightmare to read. This is especially true when a letter writer uses long, complex sentences or deals with a subject unfamiliar to the reader.

Purpose of Punctuation

Clarity should be the goal of every writer who wants the message in a letter to be understood. This goal is often lost, however, when punctuation is misused. Most abuse occurs when a writer uses complicated sentences and paragraphs, hoping to give the impression that he or she has a sophisticated, indepth understanding of a difficult topic. The ploy seldom works. For example:

> Dear Mr. Hyatt:
>
> Thank you for your inquiry about the Shields Policy. You are correct that this is a relatively new policy and it appears to be popular.
>
> I have studied the policy thoroughly, and in part, am ambivalent about it. The consensus about this coverage, is that it is a form of insurance against common losses--rather than against devasting economic disasters which is not an argument against the policy but if you already have auto coverage you might benefit from another option.
>
> I will call you next week when I am in your neighborhood to arrange a time when we can discuss this further.
>
>   Sincerely,

This example not only needs additional punctuation for clarity, but it also needs to have misplaced punctuation removed. Since the language is unnecessarily stuffy, the example can be improved further by recasting it before repunctuating it.

> Dear Mr. Hyatt:
>
> Thanks for asking about the Shields Policy. You're right that this is a relatively new policy, and it appears to be popular.
>
> I've studied the policy and, in part, have mixed feelings about it. The coverage insures you against common losses, rather than against devastating economic disasters. This does not mean that it's a bad policy. But if you already have auto coverage, you might benefit more from a different type of policy.
>
> I'll call you next week when I'm in your neighborhood to arrange a time when we can discuss this further.
>
> Cordially,

Readers who get lost in a confusing sentence or paragraph are more likely to *doubt* the writer's grasp of the subject because of his or her apparent inability to be clear and articulate. Punctuation, therefore, is crucial to effective communication, something every professional strives to achieve.

How Much Punctuation? The question is, how much is enough punctuation? Although the trend is to use less punctuation in contemporary writing, letter writers should be skeptical of this practice, particularly in the business world. In foreign correspondence, in fact, you should overpunctuate your messages, as explained in Section 52 of Chapter 6. Readers unfamiliar with the English language need to be guided through each sentence very carefully to avoid misreading it.

Even in domestic correspondence, a missing comma or other mark of punctuation can confuse a reader. To avoid that risk, a letter writer should not hesitate to use any punctuation mark as long as it is properly placed. Misplaced punctuation is another matter and can mislead a reader just as quickly as missing punctuation. (Refer to Section 56 of Chapter 7 for examples of proper punctuation in the inside address, salutation, complimentary close, and other parts of letters and memos.)

Punctuation Marks

Principal Marks of Punctuation. Grammar books usually explain the many uses and abuses of the principal marks of punctuation. The following list describes the most common uses. Proper use of these marks in your messages will contribute significantly to the professional appearance of your correspondence.

Apostrophe (')	Used to indicate the omission of a letter or letters from a word, the possessive case, and the plurals of numbers, letters, and abbreviations: *don't; company's employment policy; three R's.*
Colon (:)	Used after a word introducing a quotation, explanation, example, or a series; after the salutation in a business or social letter; and in designations of time and ratios: three types of desk calendars: (1) *daily,* (2) *weekly,* and (3) *monthly; 3:30 p.m.; 5:1 odds.*
Comma (,)	Used to indicate a separation of ideas or elements in a sentence or a pause or separation: "The question is, who is responsible?" "My wife, Jennifer, has a bookkeeping service." *Jennifer* is set off by commas

because the sentence is clear without her name—the man has only one wife. If he had been referring to one of two sons, the sentence would not be clear without stating which son, and hence the name would not be set off by commas: "My son Bill has a bookkeeping service" or "My oldest son has a bookkeeping service."

Dash (—) Used to set off parenthetical, explanatory, or other clauses; to set off a thought repeated for emphasis; or to introduce a series: "His car—the station wagon—is always having mechanical problems"; the assistants—Tom, Paul, and Sharon. The dash should be used sparingly in correspondence.

Ellipsis Points (. . .) Used to indicate the omission of words in quoted material or used as leaders in tabulations. Three points are used for material omitted in the middle or beginning of a sentence; four points are used for material omitted at the end of a sentence, with one of the points representing a period: "European unemployment grew from 14.6 million . . . to 22.0 million, as reported in *European News*. . . ." Fixed Assets...............$101,942.

Exclamation Point (!) Used to indicate emphasis, irony, or satire: "Spectacular Summer Sale!" "You broke your leg? I'll bet that was fun!" The exclamation point should be used sparingly in correspondence.

Hyphen (-) Used between the parts of a compound word or name, between a prefix and a proper noun, and

	between the syllables of a word that is divided at the end of a line: a one- to two-year independent-study program; pro-American; considera-tion.
Parentheses ( ) and Brackets [ ]	Used to enclose explanatory or qualifying words or numbers and used in mathematical expressions. When an additional expression is used within a parenthetical expression, enclose the additional expression in brackets: "This assessment is imposed on state-regulated utilities for environmental programs (e.g., to save natural resources [see Article 3] used to produce electricity) and for related programs and activities"; $[a(x-y) \times b(v+m)]$.
Period (.)	Used to indicate the end of a sentence; to separate the parts of abbreviations or show omitted letters in abbreviated words; and after a letter or numbered item in a list or outline: admin.; "He received the Sc.D. in June." 1. Parentheses and brackets.
Question Mark (?)	Used after a direct question or to indicate doubt: "Is it true?" "The letter was dated August 11(?), 1993."
Quotation Marks (' ")	Used to indicate certain titles and other quoted words. Single quotation marks are used to indicate a quotation within a quotation: the chapter "Punctuation"; The *Writer's Magazine* emphasized the public's interest in this sentence: "According to Roger Jordan, 'The pamphlet *Common Sense Scheduling* was sold out in one week.'"

Semicolon (;)	Used to connect independent clauses while indicating a closer relationship between the clauses than a period does; also used to separate a series that already contains commas: "The assimilation of iron in the system is synergistic; that is, it depends on other elements all working together"; in Concord, New Hampshire; Princeton, New Jersey; and Raleigh, North Carolina.
Virgule, Solidus, or Slash (/)	Used to separate the parts of certain abbreviations; to indicate the word *per*; and to indicate the ends of verse lines: B/L (bill of lading); 60 miles/hour; When humankind falls / Then the clocks of time shall stop.

Common Punctuation Errors. Just as you should review your correspondence for grammatical errors, you should check it for punctuation errors *before* sending it out. You may, for example, know precisely where a comma or period should or should not go, but a slip of the finger at your typewriter or computer keyboard can quickly and unintentionally add or delete a mark. Watch for other common punctuation errors too. For example:

- Periods are no longer used in organizational abbreviations: ACLU; IBM.
- A question mark should not be used when a statement is intended: "Would you please return the enclosed brochure." "Isn't that a shame."
- In American-style punctuation, periods and commas are placed inside quotation marks but colons and semicolons are not: "The instructions state that users should 'cut the felt,' roll it, and 'affix it'; the applications are 'limitless.'" The ad stated that "the theater is not responsible for lost articles": clothing, money, pens, notebooks, and so on.

- When a city and state fall in the middle of a sentence, enclose the state in commas: "I moved to Lombard, Illinois, in 1992."
- When a date in the middle of a sentence includes the month, day, and year, enclose the year in commas; otherwise, omit the comma between the month and year: "Their tenth anniversary was on March 9, 1993, about a month before yours. Our tenth anniversary was also in April 1993."
- Separate three or more items in a series with commas, including the item preceding the conjunction; use semicolons between items that already have commas: stationery, stamps, and address labels; on November 1, 1993; August 15, 1994; and March 30, 1995."

Refer to Section 14 for rules about punctuation used to divide words at the end of a line.

12. DEVELOP A MODERN CAPITALIZATION STYLE

Have you noticed what a mishmash of capitalization styles are used in the letters you receive? Not only does the style differ from one letter to another, but it also is often inconsistent within a letter.

The Perils of Inconsistency

Inconsistency is often considered the most serious offense in matters of capitalization. Most readers are forgiving of a particular style that may differ from the one they use, but they are very intolerant of a letter writer's failure to use a style consistently. They may be puzzled and confused when a term is capitalized in one sentence and not capitalized in another sentence. For example:

Dear Sam:

Yes, we completed the common business-oriented language program on July 14, and now we hope to develop a data-processing program for the support staff.

I'm happy to report that the Common Business Oriented Language Program was a huge success. Employees, in fact, have requested that it be repeated next year or that a sequel be offered.

I'll let you know if we decide to repeat the business program. Thanks for asking about it.

Best regards,

Is the writer trying to signal some important difference in interpretation by first using lowercase letters for the program name and then capitalizing it? Or is the writer simply careless? In the first instance, the reader wastes time pondering whether the difference in style means something significant. In the second instance, the reader doubts that a difference is intended but disapproves of the writer's sloppy writing and lack of professionalism.

How to Select the Right Style

Published Style Guides. Since capitalization styles differ among letter writers, a choice must be made. Writers who want to be certain they are using a widely accepted modern style may purchase a style book suitable for their personal or professional interests. Numerous style books are available in bookstores and libraries, for example, *The Elements of Style* (Macmillan) and *The Chicago Manual of Style* (University of Chicago Press). The various disciplines also have specialized guides, such as the *Style Manual* of the American Institute of Physics. Always ask for the latest edition of the style book you select.

Capitalization Rules

General Guidelines. Although a detailed style book is needed to review capitalization rules for all types of terminology, a few general guidelines apply to most letter-writing situations.

- Capitalize all important words in the inside address, salutation, and subject line of a letter:

    Mr. Jason Whorley
    101 West Avenue
    Pueblo, CO 81009

    Dear Mr. Whorley:

    SUBJECT: Real Estate Closing

- Lowercase (use small letters for) all but the first word in the complimentary close: Very cordially yours, Best regards. Refer to Section 56 in Chapter 7 for examples of proper capitalization in the various elements of letters and memos.
- Capitalize the major words in all official names and titles used in the body of a letter: University of Washington; *The Elements of Correspondence*; Mississippi River; Department of History; World War II; President Harold Fremont; First Methodist Church.
- Lowercase unofficial, general references to names and titles: the university; the correspondence book; the river; the history department; the war; the president; the church.
- Capitalize geographical regions and official names designating parts of the world: the North; Western world; Eastern Hemisphere; Far East; New York State; South Seas; the Orient; British Empire.
- Lowercase directions and unofficial, general references to areas: to the north; western states; the hemispheres; eastern Asia; state of New York; southern oceans; oriental lands; the empire.
- Capitalize the letters in acronyms, initialisms, and other abbreviations that refer to proper nouns: YMCA; IBM; JFK; SALT; BASIC.

- Lowercase most general initialisms and other abbreviations: asap; aka; ml; enc.; ft. Consult a modern book of abbreviations for numerous variations in the capitalization and punctuation of both technical and nontechnical abbreviations.

Impact on Professionalism

Letter writers sometimes forget how closely readers scrutinize a letter. Even readers who just scan a letter see a lot. It only takes a brief glance for a reader to gain an impression of your writing style. A modern capitalization style, for example, that is suitable for your personal or professional activities and is used *consistently* will readily enhance the professional appearance of your letters. But an inconsistent or outdated style will just as quickly detract from it and give the impression that you're uneducated or out of touch with the modern world.

13. IMPROVE YOUR SPELLING AS YOU WRITE

Spelling Aids

Not many letter writers are expert spellers, so you probably have a well-worn dictionary on your desk or a heavily used spell-checker in your computer. But neither spelling aid completely solves the problem.

Disadvantages of Spell-Checkers. Looking up numerous words in a dictionary every time you write a letter can become tiresome. But using a computer spell-checker has its drawbacks too. Most spell-checkers, for example, can't choose correctly between misused or sound-alike words, such as *confident* and *confidant* or *conscious* and *conscience*; nor can they determine that *its* is a typo for *it's* (it is).

Not all spell-checkers follow modern spelling trends either. Some, for example, follow the old-fashioned practice of hyphenating all prefixes. But in contemporary writing, prefixes such as *anti-, neo-, non-, post-, pre-, pro-, pseudo-,* and *semi-* are no longer hyphenated (*nonessential*), unless they precede a proper noun (*pro-European*) or unless the omission of a hyphen makes reading difficult, as in the case of a double vowel (*anti-insurance*).

Finding a Better Solution. Computer spell-checkers and printed spelling guides, such as *The Bad Spellers Book* (Random House) or *Word Traps* (Macmillan), can be very helpful. But the most satisfactory long-term solution would be to improve your spelling to the point that you need to rely on such guides less and less. One of the easiest ways to improve your spelling is to concentrate on it every time you write a letter.

Practice

Keeping a List of Difficult Words. Some writers keep a notebook or alphabetical card file on their desks in which they jot down every word they misspell or have to look up because they're uncertain how to spell it. The conscious act of recording a word seems to help implant the term into memory. You may have to write a troublesome term five or six times as an exercise, and if that isn't enough, you should regularly review the list.

Using Mnemonics. Another practical activity is *mnemonics*—a technique or phrase to help you remember something, such as how to spell a word. If, for example, you have trouble remembering whether a word such as *indispensable* ends in *-able* or *-ible*, you might try creating an easy-to-remember expression that includes the troublesome word: "An *able* employee is indispens*able*."

Commonly Misspelled Words

The traditional rules of spelling are very complex, and most of the rules have numerous exceptions that render them almost useless to most people. Instead of trying to memorize all the rules and exceptions, letter writers who are willing to work toward a goal of producing error-free correspondence might benefit more by studying the words that writing authorities have determined are especially difficult. Secretarial handbooks, spelling books, and similar business guides often have lists of such words. Here are some examples of words that are commonly misspelled:

absence	convenience	maintenance
accede	creditor	negotiate
accessible	deceive	ninety
achievement	deductible	occurrence
acknowledgment	defendant	patronage
advantageous	dependent	permissible
advisable	depositor	perseverance
allotted	deteriorate	precede
all right	discrepancy	preferable
analogous	ecclesiastical	preference
analyze	efficiency	privilege
apparel	eligible	proceed
appreciable	endeavor	prominent
assessment	equipped	questionnaire
attendance	etiquette	receipt
baccalaureate	exaggerate	recurrence
bankruptcy	exceed	regrettable
benefited	familiarize	remittance
buoyant	forcible	responsibility
casualty	fulfillment	satisfactorily
circumstances	genuine	serviceable
clientele	grievance	simultaneous
collateral	harass	sufficient
commitment	hazardous	superintendent
comparable	illegible	supersede
competent	inasmuch as	tariff
concede	incidentally	transferred
conceivable	interfere	urgent
concurred	judgment	vacuum
congratulate	legible	valuable
conscientious	liaison	vendor
consensus	license	vicinity

If spelling is one of your weak spots, any effort you make to improve it will be worthwhile. Since misspelled words in your correspondence will give readers the impression that you're careless or ignorant, correct spelling is essential to an image of professionalism.

14. USE CORRECT WORD DIVISION IN YOUR MESSAGES

Is Word Division Necessary?

We could add to the title of this section "*if* you divide words at the end of a line." Some people don't. Computer users, for example, often solve the problem of correct word division by letting the computer automatically adjust each line, without breaking any words.

Since letters are traditionally prepared unjustified, with an uneven right margin, there is (almost) nothing wrong with avoiding end-of-line word breaks altogether. However, it's important to remember that a professionally prepared message needs more than correct grammar and the absence of typos. It also must look attractive on the page, and an *exceptionally* ragged right margin is unappealing.

Notice the difference in appearance between these two examples—the first without end-of-line word division and the second with word breaks introduced to make the lines appear more even.

Dear Eileen:

   I appreciated your suggestion for
improving our procedures in processing incoming
data systems proposals. Our policy now is to
offer three alternative responses as follows:

The entry office reviews and evaluates
each new request, supporting
documentation, and system description,
recommending three alternative
responses.

I think your idea for limiting the responses to a
simple accept or reject deserves further
study. I'll talk to my boss about it and will call
you next week.

Many thanks for your help.

With best wishes,

Dear Eileen:

I appreciated your suggestion for improving
our procedures in processing incoming data systems proposals. Our policy now is to offer three
alternative responses as follows:

The entry office reviews and evaluates
each new request, supporting documentation, and system description, recommending three alternative responses.

I think your idea for limiting the responses to a
simple accept or reject deserves further study.
I'll talk to my boss about it and will call you
next week.

Many thanks for your help.

With best wishes,

In the first example, the right margin is very ragged. By
breaking three words in the second example, the right margin
looks less ragged, and the message seems to be more attractively arranged on the page. Word division, therefore, may be

necessary occasionally to maintain the professional appearance of your correspondence. (The effort could backfire, though, if you divide too many words.) Here are two helpful rules.

- A letter should not have more than two successive lines with end-of-line word breaks.
- The last word on the first page of a letter should not be divided.

How to Divide Words

Dictionary entries usually show syllables according to pronunciation (*ef-fec-tu-al*). Most of the time you can divide a word at the end of a line between any of the syllables. But exceptions do occur. For example:

- Do not divide one-syllable words, words with four or fewer letters, or abbreviations and contractions: through (*not* th-rough), into (*not* in-to), NATO (*not* NA-TO), doesn't (*not* does-n't).
- If a word has a one-letter syllable in the middle of the word, divide after that one-letter syllable (unless it is the suffix *-able* or *-ible*): busi-ness (*not* bus-iness), sepa-rate (*not* sep-arate), but consider-able (*not* considera-ble).
- If a word has a one-letter syllable at the beginning or end of the word, do not separate that letter, and try not to separate a two-letter syllable from the end of a word: about (*not* a-bout), teller (*not* tell-er).
- When the final consonant is doubled before adding a suffix to a base word, divide between the final consonant and the one that is added. But when a double consonant already exists in the base word, divide after the two like consonants: occur-ring (*not* occurr-ing), call-ing (*not* cal-ling).
- When a base word has two different consonants in succession, divide between those two consonants: foun-tain (*not* fount-ain), sen-tence (*not* sent-ence).

- When a base word has a prefix or suffix added to it, divide after the prefix or before the suffix rather than elsewhere in the base word: pre-existing (*not* preexisting), manage-ment (*not* man-agement).
- Divide a hyphenated compound word by the existing hyphen: self-examination (*not* self-examina-tion); ex-senator (*not* ex-sena-tor).
- Avoid dividing numbers, but if necessary, divide them by a comma. Divide numbers in dates between the day and year: $2,643,-912 (*not* $2,64-3,912), May 12, / 1994 (*not* May / 12, 1994).
- Divide names between first and last name, not between initials: R. J. / Bonnevaire (*not* R. / J. Bonnevaire); F. Steven Brownley (*not* F. / Steven Brownley).

Reader Comprehension. The rules of word division are intended not only to make your correspondence look attractive but also to help readers avoid misreading. If, for example, you divide the word *present* after the *s* (*pres-ent*), the reader assumes you're referring to a gift. If you divide it after the *e* (*pre-sent*), the reader assumes you mean "to give or introduce."

Any incorrect division is hard to follow. Dividing the word *transition*, for instance, as *tr-ansition*, instead of *transi-tion*, will cause a reader to stumble. Proper word division, therefore, is an important consideration as you strive to enhance the professionalism of your correspondence.

3

Getting Ready to Compose a Message

15. REREAD THE LETTER TO BE ANSWERED

Answering a letter can be more difficult than initiating the correspondence. When you write the first letter, you don't have to worry about responding to everything that the other person asked or said. Not all writers worry about this, although a thoughtful correspondent is always concerned about the other person.

Why Letter Writers Should Respond Fully

Everyone should be certain to respond fully to all points made in a letter that is being answered. If you've ever received a letter that failed to respond to some or all of your comments and questions, you'll know how annoying that failure can be. Assume, for example, that you wrote to a mail-order company with a specific question about a product you would like to order.

> Ladies and Gentlemen:
>
> Are custom orders accepted by Gifts 'n' More? I am interested in a small brass table that appears on page 17 of the fall issue of

your catalog (no. H713-09, $79.98). Would it be
possible to custom-order this table in either
chrome or black enamel?

   Please let me know if either of those finishes
is available by custom order, and send prices and
instructions for placing the order.

   Thank you for your help.

                                        Sincerely,

   Now, assume that after sending that letter you received the
following reply.

   Dear Customer:

      Thank you for your recent inquiry about our
   merchandise. We are happy to enclose a copy of
   our latest catalog where you will find many
   quality products now available at low factory
   prices.

      We very much appreciate your interest in our
   merchandise and hope you will let us know if you
   have any questions. Thank you for writing to
   Gifts 'n' More.

                                        Cordially,

   It's obvious that the person receiving the inquiry paid no
attention to the specific question that was asked. Perhaps the
recipient hastily scanned the letter, noticed that it contained a
question about a catalog product, and decided that an easy
way to respond would be to send the writer a form letter and
a copy of the most recent catalog. Although this may have
been a simple way to dispose of incoming mail, it also may
have irritated the customer enough to prompt him or her to
look for the chrome or black table elsewhere.

The Importance of Rereading Letters

Busy people are reluctant to spend a lot of time rereading the letters they receive, but the time needed to do this is well spent. In business it is essential to respond fully, or sales may be lost. In personal matters, too, it is only common courtesy to respond fully to the comments and questions you receive. After all, no one likes to be ignored. The only way people know whether you bothered to read their letters is if you respond to the content when you reply.

If you answer a letter immediately upon receipt of it, the chances of forgetting to reply to something are minimal. But if time elapses, the chances of forgetting some point will increase. A basic guideline is: never trust your memory. Reread each letter you receive before you answer it. Then follow the suggestions in Sections 16 through 19 before you actually start writing.

16. HIGHLIGHT THE MAIN POINTS

Highlighting the main points of a letter you are answering or listing the main points you want to make in a letter you are initiating may sound like a high school exercise. It isn't. Many professional businesspeople, in fact, have made it a habit to do exactly that. Professionals know that it's important to answer letters completely (see Section 15) and to present the points they want to make clearly and logically.

Highlighting in a Letter Received

How to Highlight Main Points. No firm rule exists about how you should highlight the main points in a letter you receive. Some letter writers use yellow marking pens, some underline key words or sentences, and others jot notes in the margins of the incoming letter.

In personal correspondence, you can use any such method that appeals to you. In business correspondence, however, you'll be expected to follow office policy about writing on original letters. Some organizations don't allow any marking on incoming letters, and you may then want to write a few notes on a separate slip of paper, such as a self-sticking note, and attach it to the letter to be answered.

Some people believe it saves time to highlight main points in an incoming letter while reading it for the first time. Others prefer to do this while rereading the letter, just before composing a reply. In this example of a letter received, the person replying highlighted the words that are shown here in italics.

Dear Mr. Walton:

Thank you for inviting me to *serve on* the Constitution and Bylaws *Committee*.

I appreciate the opportunity to work with all of you and can give you a *qualified yes*. I will be away on business from June 1 to August 1 and *would have to miss meetings scheduled in June and July*. Would that be *acceptable*?

I'll look forward to your decision, Mr. Walton. If you believe that this absence would be too long, I'll certainly understand.

Thanks for thinking of me.

Regards,

How to List the Main Points. If you would prefer not to mark on the letter, you could attach a slip of paper or self-sticking note listing the key points you want to keep in mind as you reply. Use any form of abbreviation or shorthand that is understandable to you, such as the following:

1. Qualified yes to serve on CBC
2. Would miss Jun-Jul meetings
3. Decide if okay

Listing Points in a Letter Initiated

If you are writing the first letter—that is, if you are not reply-ing to an existing letter—you obviously wouldn't have any-thing from someone else to highlight. In this case, you could simply list the main points that you want to make in your let-ter, using any form of abbreviation that is understandable to you. Assume that you want to order two theater tickets to a play in a nearby city. Your brief notes might look like this.

1. "Hurricane," March 7, 8 p.m.
2. 2 mezzanine seats
3. P.U. at box office, Mar 7, afternoon
4. Ck., $90, enclosed
5. Sase enclosed

Your letter, with these notes as a guide, might then be com-posed as follows.

> Ladies and Gentlemen:
>
> Please reserve two mezzanine seats for the March 7 performance of "Hurricane" at 8 p.m. My check for $90 is enclosed. I will pick up the tickets at your box office on the afternoon of March 7.
>
> Please let me know which seats are being reserved and confirm that the two tickets will be available for pickup on March 7. A stamped, self-addressed envelope is enclosed for your convenience in replying.
>
> Thank you.
>
> Sincerely,

Some letters require research before or after the main points are listed. The next section discusses the collection of information for a more complex letter, and Sections 18 and 19 describe organizational procedures when more detail is involved.

17. Collect the Information You Will Need

Most of the letters you will write may be relatively simple. You may already know all the facts you will use—times, dates, names, addresses, instructions, statistics, and other specific data. Usually, though, when a letter includes important details, the writer needs to look up or verify at least some of the information. A letter with imprecise facts can be misleading and is likely to irritate the reader. Imagine, for instance, receiving this letter.

Dear Jamie:

Yes, the optics seminar you asked about would be useful. Please make arrangements to attend.

I think it will be held in Wisconsin or Michigan sometime in October or November. It probably will last two or three days, possibly four. The fee is going to be about $50 or $60. There may be other costs too. Although I don't have the sponsor's address, I believe the organization is located in Wisconsin.

I hope you enjoy the seminar. Let me know if I can help with your registration and travel arrangements.

Best wishes,

As you can see, the writer offered only one concrete piece of information—the authorization for Jamie to attend the seminar. The rest of the facts are so vague that they are almost useless. The writer should have collected the necessary information before responding or should have instructed someone else to do so.

Researching a Letter

Sources of Information. Different letters deal with different topics, so the information-collection procedure may vary from one letter to another. In some cases, you may find the facts you need in a book, magazine, newsletter, newspaper, or report. A telephone call or a meeting with a friend or associate may also produce the information you need. Or you may use your computer to retrieve the required information from a database.

Collecting the Information. The writer of the letter in the previous example could have inquired around the office or checked a directory for the precise name, address, and telephone number of the organization sponsoring the seminar. A telephone call to the sponsor, with a written list of questions to refer to, probably would have provided the facts needed to be clear and specific in the letter of authorization. For example, the writer could have asked the following preliminary questions by telephone and at the same time requested that further details be sent by mail.

- Name, address, and telephone number of sponsor
- Title of seminar
- Location of seminar
- Date of seminar
- Registration fee and other costs
- Travel and accommodations information

With this preliminary information, the writer could have composed a more intelligent reply to Jamie.

Dear Jamie:

Yes, the optics seminar you asked about would
be useful. Please make arrangements to attend.

The seminar, "Optics Today," is being
sponsored by the Optics Association, 2100 North
End Avenue, Marshfield, Wisconsin 54404, Phone
715-555-6309. It is scheduled for October 8-10,
1994, at the Royal Hotel in Marshfield. The
registration fee for the three days is $60. Travel,
hotel accommodations, meals, and entertainment
costs are additional, and arrangements for these
items are the responsibility of the attendees. I've
requested that complete program and registration
details be sent to both of us.

I hope you enjoy the seminar. Let me know if I
can help with your registration and travel
arrangements.

Best wishes,

The final sections in this chapter discuss other steps that
may be necessary when a letter involves greater detail or a
more complex subject.

18. Organize the Main Facts

Although you can mentally organize the information used in
a brief, simple message, you will need to organize the main
facts in a longer, more complex message on a piece of paper
or on your computer screen. If you don't arrange your comments in a clear, logical progression, you may forget something or you may confuse the reader.

A complex letter that contains a lot of important factual information should be treated like a report or an article. If you think of a letter in this way, the chief topic or topics that you plan to discuss must be researched and all important information examined before you compose the letter. The main points of the letter must then be arranged in order of importance in a way that will advance the purpose of your message.

If an outline is prepared, it can be used as a blueprint when you write the first rough draft of your letter. Refer to Section 19 for a description of an outline prepared for a complex letter and Section 20 in Chapter 4 for an example of a rough draft prepared from an outline.

How to Organize the Main Facts

Assume that you work for a real estate firm that will be publishing a small booklet to be called *Buying Your Own Home.* The booklet will be passed out to prospective customers who have indicated an interest in owning their own home. You have received a letter from the manager of the firm, asking for specific suggestions on what to include in the booklet, and you want the manager to be impressed with your letter.

Organizing the Key Topics. As you begin reviewing books, articles, and other real estate material that has been published and as you discuss the matter with others in the office, you may notice that certain topics, such as location of the property, are repeated over and over. Such prevalent information would be ideal as main topics in the real estate firm's proposed booklet.

At this early stage, if you don't know enough about the subject to develop a detailed outline, you will be jotting down information as you read it, without regard to any orderly plan for your letter. (Use any form of shorthand that suits you.)

Assume now that you believe you have jotted down the major topics that you want to suggest to the manager in your letter. But after looking at your notes, you realize that the topics are not listed in any logical order. After several attempts at reorganizing your rough notes, you may settle for this arrangement of topics.

- Advantages of ownership—tax savings, equity, security of not having to move, personal choices in decorating
- Disadvantages of ownership—property taxes, upkeep, must wait to sell before moving
- What the real estate broker does—provides information on location and other details, helps arrange financing, answers questions, handles closing
- Deciding on a location—neighborhood, schools, hospitals, churches, stores, public transportation, septic-sewer system, noise and other pollution, crime, roads, zoning and other restrictions, fire and police protection, garbage pickup, snow removal, parking
- Deciding how much to spend—mortgage = a maximum of 29% of monthly gross income
- Mortgage loans—application, period of loan, principal, interest, homeowner's insurance, property tax, assumable mortgages, FHA-insured mortgages
- Loan options—fixed-rate mortgage (stable payments but higher interest), adjustable-rate mortgage (lower payments at first but unpredictable rate over time)
- Down payment—amount (typically 10–20%—HUD homes less) and when due
- Advantages of HUD homes—lower down payments, HUD may pay closing costs and broker's commission
- Inspection—roof, plumbing, electrical, structural soundness, final walk-through
- The closing—expenses, papers to sign, and so on

The notes, however, are still just that—notes. Although the topics are generally arranged in a logical order for the letter, each main topic has a number of subtopics, and you may be uncertain whether the subtopics are listed logically. Also, as you look at the notes, you may wonder whether some of the main topics should be combined. The topics in the notes appear to need further refinement before expanding them into readable paragraphs of a letter. Section 19 illustrates one way to take the main facts and rearrange them in the form of an outline.

19. DEVELOP AN OUTLINE FOR YOUR MESSAGE

Advantages of Outlining a Message

Outlining the main points of a complex message helps letter writers to visualize the clarity, completeness, and logical arrangement of their comments. The information should be discussed in a particular order that will help the reader understand it and reach a certain conclusion.

Limiting the Number of Subtopic Levels

An *outline*—a numbered or lettered list of topics that also contains numbered or lettered subtopics—can be as simple or as intricate as you want to make it. Usually, though, a two- or three-level outline is sufficient for a letter.

If a topic involves not only subtopics but also numerous levels of sub-subtopics, it probably needs to be simplified to make it more suitable for discussion in a letter. If a topic is so complex that it can't be simplified to just two or three levels, it would be better to develop the information as a supplementary report and send it with a brief cover letter explaining the enclosure.

How to Prepare an Outline

Use of Numbers and Letters. You may use any outlining style that appeals to you. Although you might prefer a more detailed outline, with numerous sublevels, the example in this section consists of main topics (A, B, and so on) and first-level subtopics (1, 2, and so on).

How to List the Topics on an Outline. Although some writers like to use full sentences that can later be used as opening sentences in the paragraphs of their letters, it is more common to use brief descriptions for topics and subtopics.

If you arrange your rough notes in a logical order (see Section 18), it will simplify the outlining process, because the order of the main topics of the outline will be similar to the order of the main facts in the notes. Nevertheless, it is common to make still further refinements during outlining.

The sample outline in this section is based on the notes that were collected for Section 18. In the outline, the letter writer reduced the number of major topics indicated in the notes by combining certain similar topics and omitting others. But the writer added other topics. Such content changes can be made more easily in the outline stage than during the actual composition stage.

A. Owning your own home
   1. Advantages
   2. Disadvantages
B. Using a real estate broker
   1. How a broker operates
   2. What a broker does
C. Selecting a home
   1. The neighborhood
   2. The house
D. Financing a home
   1. Deciding how much to spend
   2. Mortgage loans
   3. Rate options
E. Closing on a home
   1. Inspection before closing
   2. The closing

When you're satisfied that your outline includes all topics you want to mention in your letter in the order you want to mention them, you're ready to write the first rough draft of the letter—the subject of Section 20 in the next chapter.

4

Composing the Message

20. PREPARE A FIRST DRAFT

The saying that amateurs write and professionals rewrite applies to correspondence as well as to other types of writing. Not many people can create a perfect letter in one draft, but having notes or an outline to guide the composition can greatly reduce the amount of required revision.

Composing a Short, Simple Letter

Most short, simple messages are composed without notes or with only a few facts available at the time of writing. This simple acknowledgment letter, for instance, could be written without prior research other than rereading the incoming letter from Ms. Rainey.

> Dear Ms. Rainey:
>
> Thank you for sending a resume and letting us know that you would like to find a position as computer operator in our Word Processing Department. Daniel Fries in the Personnel Office would be happy to discuss current job opportunities with you.

Please telephone me at 555-2908 to arrange a date for you to meet with Mr. Fries. Thank you.

Sincerely,

Simple, brief business letters like this and most personal and social letters are composed with minimal or no prior information collection. Often, in fact, the same pattern is followed in many letters, with changes only in names and other miscellaneous facts and figures.

Composing a Long, Complex Letter

The more facts that a letter contains, the more important prior research becomes. Composing a complex letter with a lot of detail can seldom be done from memory. Although some people can retain huge amounts of information, professionals are reluctant to risk making an error by trusting their memory rather than double-checking facts and figures.

Preparing the First Draft. Referring to an outline while composing a relatively complex letter will help you to make your points in a logical order and lessen the chances that you will forget an important point. It will also help you to create a good first draft that may need only minor refinement rather than extensive rewriting. The following letter is an example of a first draft prepared from the outline developed in Section 19.

Dear Mrs. Flesch:

Here are the topic suggestions you requested for the proposed booklet Buying Your Own Home. My library research and conversations with others in the office have persuaded me that these topics could form the basis of chapters or other major divisions in the booklet.

Owning Your Own Home. This introductory topic should focus on the important advantages of home ownership.

Using a Real Estate Broker. This topic should clearly explain how a brokerage operates and what a broker does.

Selecting a Home. This topic should advise prospective buyers on what to look for in the neighborhood and in the house itself. (This type of information could be provided in the form of checklists.)

Financing a Home. This topic should provide the information all home buyers need about financing, mortgages, and rate options.

Closing on a Home. This topic should explain what is involved in the preclosing inspection of the property and the closing itself.

Please let me know if you'd like any additional information, Mrs. Flesch. I enjoyed the assignment very much and would be happy to participate further in the production of the booklet.

Sincerely,

Ideally, after preparing a first draft, you would set the letter aside for a short time and return to it later with a fresh outlook. If that isn't possible, you will have to rely on your ability to search immediately for errors, omissions, poorly phrased statements, and other problems. The rest of this chapter describes other factors, such as tone and word choice, that determine the effectiveness of a letter and need to be considered when reviewing and revising a first rough draft.

21. VISUALIZE YOUR READER

Developing a Portrait of the Reader

Creating a mental profile of your reader is an essential exercise if you want to write a successful letter. Visualizing the reader is easy when you write to family, friends, or coworkers that you know very well. It's not so easy when you write to someone you've never met.

Why You Should Analyze Readers

The reason for learning as much as you can about your readers is that you want your letters to be understood and appreciated. Your comments are more likely to be appropriate if you know something about the person's education; personal, social, and professional environment; interests; and personality. For example:

- Does the person have enough training to understand any technical descriptions you need to provide?
- Does the person like or dislike humor in a letter?
- Does the person like or dislike numerous details in a letter?

People are complex beings, and it would be easy to unwittingly say something in a letter that might be appropriate for one person but very inappropriate for someone else. An inappropriate comment could offend or annoy a reader, and this in turn might cause the person to respond negatively to something you are saying or proposing. It's difficult to imagine a situation in which you would want to hurt or anger a reader intentionally. Much more is to be gained by making someone feel good.

When You Don't Know the Reader. In business it's often necessary to write to people you don't know. In such cases, avoid controversial subjects, and if it serves no purpose to be critical or to espouse a particular viewpoint, don't do it. Stick to the purpose of the letter and make your remarks generally acceptable to people of different personal, social, and professional backgrounds.

Assume, for example, that you are sending a cover letter with a brochure that promotes some new computer software. All you know is that the reader wrote to ask for information, so he or she apparently is somewhat interested in computer-related matters. Without knowing more, however, it would be a mistake and could appear sexist to guess at the person's gender.

"Every *man* in your position should have this software."

It would also be a mistake to guess about other reader characteristics, such as the person's educational level.

"As a *college graduate,* you will appreciate this state-of-the-art software."

Perhaps the person who asked for information is a woman and someone who either never went to college or graduated a long time ago. Or perhaps someone's grandmother wants to give her grandchild some software for the child's birthday. Whenever doubt exists, rephrase your comments to be neutral:

"*Anyone* who uses a computer at home or at work will appreciate this software."

In most cases, you can personalize a letter without guessing about the person's gender or other reader characteristics.

"If *you* use a computer at home or at work, *you* will appreciate this software."

Examples of Reader Characteristics. Here are examples of reader characteristics that could affect what you say in a letter and how you say it.

Age	Social status
Gender	Racial or ethnic background
Marital status	Economic status
Children	Occupation
Place of residence	Political affiliation
Disability or illness	Educational background
Religious beliefs	Interests and hobbies

Expand this list of characteristics as necessary for each reader and each situation. If you are writing to someone in another country, for example, you would also want to know something about the person's English-language skills.

When possible, increase your awareness of each individual characteristic. In certain situations, it could be helpful just to know that someone is affiliated with the Republican, Democratic, or other party, but it might be even more helpful to know that the person is a leader or activist in the party. In the same way, it could be useful to know that someone's hobby is golf, but it might be even more useful to know that the person is a pro golfer or arranges tournaments. An important rule to remember is that the more you know about a person, the more intelligently you can comment to that person in your letters.

22. TAKE THE "YOU" APPROACH

The "you" approach in letter writing is a very effective psychological technique for focusing on the reader and the reader's interests. Instead of approaching everything from the selfish perspective of *I*, *we*, and *our*, a letter writer approaches subjects from the viewpoint of the reader and makes this clear by frequently using the word *you*.

Objective of the "You" Approach

The objective in using the "you" approach is to treat the reader in each letter as the most important person in the world and to demonstrate that what you are thinking, saying, or doing has the reader's best interest in mind. But all comments must sound honest and sincere. Applying the "you" approach merely as a clever device or a gimmick intended only to deceive and trick the reader into believing something false is likely to fail—and it should.

Using the "You" Approach

When to Use the "You" Approach. Use the "you" approach in domestic correspondence in these cases:

- When you want to be friendly and conversational.
- When you want to show concern for the reader.
- When you want to stimulate a positive response to you and your letters.

You can contribute to all of these goals by writing about things of interest to the reader and by making clear that the points of your letter are of significance to the reader.

When Not to Use the "You" Approach. Don't use the "you" approach in these cases:

- When the reader lives in a country where people object to emphasizing individuals over organizations. In some countries, such as Japan, the company is considered more important than the individual. Refer to Chapter 6 for tips on writing international messages.
- When you want to avoid criticizing or blaming someone for something. Instead of writing "*You* made an error in the first paragraph," say "An error appears in the first paragraph."

How to Adopt the "You" Approach. If you're not accustomed to writing about things of interest to the reader or phrasing your comments to show the significance of them to the reader, you can practice revising your messages until the "you" attitude becomes nearly automatic. The next two business letters illustrate how to do this. The first letter is written from the viewpoint of the writer, not the reader, and emphasizes the writer's views and interests. Notice how selfish it sounds with such heavy use of *we* and *our*.

Welcome!

> We are happy to enclose the first issue of our new <u>Future Health Letter</u>. We think that subscribing to this letter is one of the wisest routes to good health both today and tomorrow.

> We believe that prevention is the key to future wellness, and our goal is to provide up-to-the-minute information on developments that will help millions of readers achieve and maintain good health.

> We urge our subscribers to remember that good health depends on good living--every day. That's why reading each issue of our <u>Future Health Letter</u> is the first important step to good health--the rest is up to our subscribers.

> We hope this is only the beginning for all of our <u>Future Health Letter</u> readers.

> Congratulations--and welcome!

> Sincerely,

Here's a revised version of the letter that shifts the focus to the reader.

Welcome!

> Here's your first copy of our new <u>Future Health Letter</u>. By becoming a charter subscriber, you've shown that you care about your health not only today but tomorrow.

You already know that prevention is the
key to future wellness, and the principal goal
of the Future Health Letter is to give you
up-to-the-minute information on developments
that will help you achieve and maintain good
health.

Your decision to become a charter subscriber
also shows that you know how much good health
depends on good living--every day. That's why
reading each issue of the Future Health Letter is
the first important step to good health--the rest
is up to you.

We hope this is only the beginning of your
journey to good health.

Congratulations--and welcome!

Sincerely,

The "you" approach is just as important in social and personal letters as it is in business letters and memos. Notice how self-centered the writer of this personal letter sounds.

Dear Harry,

What's new?

Sorry I didn't answer your last letter sooner,
but I've been really busy. I got a promotion
last month, and as the new manager of the
automotive section, I have a ton of new duties.

Ben and Jennie are also keeping me busy.
They're doing fine in school. Jennie, in fact, was
just asked to join the chorus, and Ben is secretary
on the Student Council.

We love our new BMW. Everyone should own
one at least once in a lifetime.

Kate is working on a new project, so she's
busy too.

Hope all is well there. Have a good Labor Day weekend.

Best,

Poor Harry. His friend was supposed to be answering his letter, but every paragraph emphasizes *I* and *we*, with nothing about the friend. Here's a rewrite that shifts to the "you" approach.

Dear Harry,

It was great to get your letter and hear what all of you have been doing this summer. Sorry I've taken so long to reply.

You must really be busy at the office. No wonder you've been feeling tired--working until 7 and 8 o'clock every evening. Your company is lucky to have you running the plant. I may have to put in a few long days too, since last month I was given a different job managing the automotive section.

It's wonderful that your kids are having so much fun in Little League. I hope you won't be too busy at work to see a few games. Ben and Jennie are busy too--Ben as secretary of the Student Council and Jennie as a new member of the chorus.

Congratulations to Deanne for being elected to the school board. She'll do a terrific job. I've always admired her dedication to school activities. Kate is still busy at work and will be heading a new project this coming year.

Keep in touch, Harry. I hope all of you have a wonderful Labor Day weekend.

Best,

Composing letters with a "you" attitude is surprisingly easy. It's easier, in fact, than adopting a formal, impersonal style.

23. BE YOURSELF

The "Dr. Jekyll and Mr. Hyde" Letter Writer

Have you ever received a letter from someone you know that sounded as though it came from a stranger? Something happens to certain people when they try to write a letter—a Dr. Jekyll-Mr. Hyde personality transfer occurs.

Why People Appear to Be Someone Else. Some writers intentionally try to sound more formal, more authoritative, or more knowledgeable than they really are in person. Although it may seem undesirable to create a false image, letters are often used to create a certain impression for very good reasons. For example:

- You may usually be a very casual, friendly person but want to sound more formal and reserved when writing to someone you don't know, someone in a high position, or someone in another country where formality is expected.
- You may have weak language skills in general but want to appear more professional and accomplished in your letters.
- You may be accustomed to talking to people who are educated or trained in the same subjects as you but want to explain something in a letter to someone who has much less understanding.
- You may have strong likes and dislikes but want your letters to give the impression that you are reasonable, open-minded, and receptive to all viewpoints.
- You may generally be very easygoing and flexible but want to build a strong, persuasive argument in a letter.

People have many different reasons for almost becoming another person in their letters. Sometimes the change occurs simply because a person feels uncomfortable writing letters, and this mental block causes stiff, awkward prose. Sometimes it happens because a person can't seem to express on paper what he or she really feels, and as a result, comments may appear unusually bland or harsh.

How to Make Your Letters Sound Like You

Not all letter writers want to be or should be themselves. A usually sour individual, for example, should not allow the tendency to be cold and unfriendly affect the tone of a letter to an important customer. But in most cases, it's best to be yourself. This advice, however, does not mean that you shouldn't be careful about your grammar or that you shouldn't try to improve other aspects of your correspondence.

Emphasize Your Best Qualities. Before you compose your next letter, take time to look inward. What kind of person are you? Considerate? Impatient? Friendly? Withdrawn? Find your best qualities and, as you compose each letter, let those qualities show. But also pinpoint your worst qualities and try just as hard *not* to let them show.

In the next example, a generally friendly person had a bad day and let her worst qualities take over. The result is a curt, cranky message that makes the normally pleasant person seem like someone else.

TO: Lillian Swartz

FROM: Jill Singleton

CURRENT BIOGRAPHY AND PHOTO

I received your updated biography today, but because you failed to enclose a current photo as requested, I was forced to delay publication of our next <u>Executive Bulletin</u>.

Please send the photo by Friday, June 11. Thank you.

Would you believe that the writer of the next letter is a fun-loving uncle writing to his favorite niece? From the stiff, formal tone, you might think that the two hardly knew each other.

> Dear Michelle,
>
>   Aunt Hattie and I want to thank you for the interesting book on houseplants. We were impressed with the photography and the detailed descriptions. I am confident that the book will prove useful in our indoor gardening activities.
>
>   We are grateful for the time and effort you devoted to selecting this gift and want to express our deepest appreciation for your thoughtfulness.
>
>   Sincerely yours,

To make your letters sound as if *you* wrote them, try writing your first draft the same way you would talk to the reader in ordinary conversation. Then edit the draft to correct grammatical errors and other weaknesses. But retain the good qualities—friendliness, compassion, attentiveness, and so on—that reflect the best in you.

24. BE SINCERE AND NATURAL

Can You Be Both Sincere and Natural?

You may wonder how anyone could possibly follow all the suggestions in this book and still sound sincere and natural in a letter. On the one hand, you're advised to be friendly, gracious, and considerate. On the other hand, you're advised to be yourself, but perhaps you don't feel friendly, gracious, and considerate. Can you, therefore, be sincere and natural at the same time? Yes, but you may have to work at it.

The Difference between Correspondence and Conversation. Any doubts about contradictory suggestions melt when you consider that differences clearly do exist between talking to someone and writing a letter to someone. Certain requirements apply to correspondence that may not be pertinent in a face-to-face meeting.

When you're talking to someone, you can often judge by the person's expression whether he or she likes or dislikes or understands or misunderstands your attitude, language, and opinions. If you notice any doubts, you can quickly restate something and keep doing so until the person responds as you expect. In a letter, though, you have to be more careful and craft your message to be certain that your words and writing style will prompt the reader response that you want. You won't be there to rephrase something if there's a problem. So you may not be as natural on paper as you would be in person.

How to Be Sincere and Natural in Correspondence

Don't Exaggerate. Any exaggeration is likely to sound phony. If you state, for example, that a certain ointment will enable people with baldness problems to grow a full head of hair overnight, no one is going to believe you. Your comments have to be believable for your readers to think that you're sincere. The same principle applies to other statements of excess, such as being overly gushy or too complimentary. For example, would you believe that the writer of this letter is being sincere and natural?

Dear Marlene,

   It was absolutely marvelous to see you at lunch yesterday. I have <u>so</u> missed our visits.

As usual, you looked positively gorgeous. I simply adore your new hair style. It is <u>so</u> glamorous. And how do you stay so young? The rest of us old hags keep getting older, and you seem to be getting younger! Bless you!

I hope we can meet soon again. I'll die if we can't have lunch soon. You're the most interesting and talented and successful person I know. I can't wait to hear more about what you've been doing.

<u>Call me</u> when you can.

Much love,

As you can see, the writer gushes and flatters a little too much—enough to cause a reader to doubt the writer's sincerity.

Don't Use Stilted Expressions. Most people don't use very formal trite expressions, such as *I wish to advise*, in conversation and wouldn't sound natural if they used them in correspondence. Section 43 in Chapter 5 has a list of stilted, outdated expressions that should be avoided in correspondence. All of them create an uncomfortable, unnatural tone in a letter.

Don't Use Pretentious Language. Pompous words and expressions, such as *vicissitude*, are as bad as trite expressions. They create the impression that the writer is showing off, and pretentious people are usually considered insincere. Section 44 in Chapter 5 has a list of pompous expressions that should be avoided in correspondence.

Don't Be too Formal. Although a more reserved writing style is necessary in international correspondence (see Chapter 6), it sounds unnatural in domestic correspondence because people usually speak informally. Not many people nowadays would phrase their comments like this in ordinary conversation:

"Indeed, it is with the greatest pleasure that I accept your kind invitation to address the Business Club of Birmingham."

If you were talking on the telephone today, you would probably respond something like this:

"Yes, I'd be happy to address the Business Club of Birmingham. Thanks very much for asking me."

Your domestic letters, therefore, should more closely resemble contemporary conversation than the formal prose of the 1800s and early 1900s.

Don't Use Cumbersome, Awkward Sentences. Sometimes we use cumbersome, awkward sentences in both speech and correspondence, and it's ineffective in both cases. This lengthy comment, for example, is too clumsy and cumbersome to seem natural.

"Demands may be initiated by a businessperson stationed abroad for products of higher quality, and this may result in a series of counterproductive measures moving down the foreign nation's hierarchy, which points to the need for even simple requests to be evaluated for their far-reaching ramifications."

Awkward sentences seem even more glaring in correspondence than in speech because the reader doesn't hear pauses or emphasis that might help in speech and, particularly, because the reader can physically see the mangled prose.

Sections 9 and 10 in Chapter 2 describe the proper use of language and good grammar in letters. Section 42 in Chapter 5 describes the problems in using jargon, buzzwords, and gobbledygook.

Review Your Correspondence

Reread some of your letters and memos and ask yourself whether the comments really sound sincere and natural.

Would a reader find them believable? Do your comments sound awkward and forced? Put yourself in the reader's place and practice rephrasing sentences that might appear insincere and unnatural to someone else. The following sections in this chapter have additional tips on other ways to improve your composition.

25. KEEP AN OPEN MIND

Whether you're writing a personal, social, or business letter, your message will be more favorably received if you listen to the reader and can make it clear in your letter that you have an open mind. Keeping an open mind is in everyone's best interest. At the least, it's a good way to impress others with your concern and fairness. No one likes to deal with people who are unwilling to consider the ideas of others, and most readers can quickly spot someone who has a closed mind.

Why a Closed Mind Is So Obvious

People who have a closed mind never seem to hear what the other person is saying. They persistently cling to their own views and usually prejudge everything before hearing all sides. This weakness is often obvious in letters, as illustrated here. The first letter contains a suggestion, and the second letter is a response from someone whose mind is apparently closed to any type of change.

Dear George:

Thanks for your memo requesting items for the October agenda.

Although I don't have any items to offer, I want to show you a fill-in agenda-topic form that we use in our Retailers Club. As you can see on the enclosed copy, the form makes it easy to circle or check off standard items and simply pencil in other items under appropriate headings such as "Committee Reports."

Since people don't have to compose and type or print out a letter and list of topics from scratch, they'll be more inclined to submit items in advance rather than unexpectedly bring them up at the meeting after the agenda has already been completed.

Feel free to use the enclosed form if you think it will help. No permission is necessary.

Best regards,

Dear Gene:

I appreciated seeing the fill-in agenda form that you sent but believe our present system works just fine. Thanks anyway for the suggestion.

Regards,

One can't help but feel that George's mind was closed or he would have been more complimentary and appreciative. If his mind had been open, he at least might have said that he would like to think about it.

Learn to Listen

Why People Fail to Listen. People are often so concerned about what they want to say or do that they fail to listen to others. Most of the time this failure is unintentional. Sometimes, though, people are afraid of being wrong or having to admit that they're wrong. Sometimes, too, they dread the time and effort that may be involved if they have to accept a different idea or a change in plans.

Why an Open Mind Is Essential. Successful people keep their eyes, ears, and minds open. Sometimes the ideas of others are not only worth hearing, they are also worth adopting even if in modified form. Even when they have serious doubts about something, open-minded people try to avoid slamming doors on other people's opinions. People like to think that they're being heard and appreciated, and it's very important to let this type of openness and concern for the views of others show in your correspondence. Notice the difference from the previous example in this reply to Gene.

Dear Gene:

I really appreciated seeing the fill-in agenda form that you sent. It appears to be very well organized and is easy to follow.

I'd like to talk to a few people in the department and ask them if they would prefer using this type of form. I know that some people love simple fill-in forms whereas others hate them.

I'll let you know the results, Gene. In the meantime, thanks so much for your thoughtfulness in sending me a copy of the form.

Regards,

The next section has more to say about adopting a reasonable attitude in correspondence.

26. BE REASONABLE

You've probably heard this saying: "When other people's opinions differ from mine, they're being unreasonable; when my opinions differ from theirs, I'm making an informed judgment." It's human nature to want everyone else to be reasonable, but not everyone is willing to accept the same standard. When this happens, it can become a glaring weakness in any correspondence that includes opinions or decisions.

What Being Reasonable Means

Being reasonable means having sound judgment and being fair. Some people think that being reasonable also means giving up too much. But it doesn't. Being reasonable, for example, *doesn't* mean:

- That you can't express firm beliefs or expectations in your letters
- That you have to modify your deepest beliefs or take steps that you know are dangerous and destructive just to demonstrate how reasonable you are
- That you have to compromise your basic moral and ethical values and standards

Being reasonable *does* mean that each time you write to someone, you need to recognize and appreciate the opinions, beliefs, abilities, and limitations of the reader. If you let your appreciation and compassion for the reader's position show in your messages, you can express a contrary view or make a different decision without damaging the relationship.

Writing under Stress

People who have a lot of stress at home or at work are sometimes impatient and tolerant, and such feelings are likely to show in their letters. Since many people experience some form of stress every day, it isn't always practical to postpone letter-writing tasks until a more stress-free time. A stress-free time might never come.

Why Stress Makes People Unreasonable. Some people are naturally unreasonable, stress or not. In general, though, letter writers need to recognize that they're not performing at their best when they're under stress. People who are under stress, however, don't always realize that they're being unreasonable, and sometimes they're so tired that they just don't care. In either case, a penalty has to be paid. The goodwill of the reader may be lost, the reader may form a poor opinion of the writer, and the negative aspect of an unreasonable position may make it difficult to accomplish anything positive.

Adopt a Reasonable Attitude

In this next example, a stressed-out sales manager was growing impatient and angry while waiting for important information from a field representative.

> Dear Brian:
>
> As you know, I've been working on our quarterly report and have been waiting for your regional call summary. In case I didn't make it clear before, let me repeat: I <u>have</u> to have this information to finish the report. Do you have a problem with this?
>
> I'll expect the call summary on my desk by Friday, the 10th.
>
> Sincerely,

Although the manager has every right to request the information by a certain date, his tone is combative and unreasonable. Since the field representative may have a legitimate reason for the delay, or the information may already be in the mail, the manager should give the employee the benefit of the doubt for now. If further investigation reveals that a reprimand is in order, that can come later.

Failure to consider or appreciate the reader's position in the previous letter makes the comments seem much too harsh. Creating antagonistic relations by being unreasonable will not contribute to a cooperative, productive relationship. The next version would be much more effective.

> Dear Brian:
>
> In checking my calendar today, I notice that our quarterly report is due on November 14. Although the deadline is near, I should be able to complete the report on time if I receive your call summary by November 10.
>
> Since we don't have much time, you may want to fax the information to me. If you're having any problems, however, please telephone me right away. Together, I'm sure we can find a quick solution so that the quarterly report won't be late.
>
> Thanks, Brian.
>
> Regards,

This version sticks to the deadline of November 10 but takes a more reasonable position rather than assume—perhaps incorrectly—that the employee had no legitimate excuse for the delay. The same reasonable approach should be used in personal letters. Before clinging stubbornly to a particular opinion or commenting angrily without knowing all the facts, take time to understand the reader's position, and let this understanding show in your message. Even if you don't change your requirements, an indication of sympathetic understanding will make you seem like a sensible, fair, and reasonable person.

27. BECOME A DIPLOMAT

Ideally, all letter writers would be diplomats and have a keen sense of how to make appropriate statements and requests that maintain good relations. All too often, however, the opposite occurs. Letter writers sometimes intentionally or, more often, unintentionally, annoy or offend the reader.

Writing Diplomatically

Being reasonable, the subject of Section 26, is a necessary ingredient, but diplomacy involves much more. To be a diplomat in correspondence, you must know how to phrase delicate and controversial matters tactfully. You must also learn how to say other things at the right time in the right way so that the reader feels good, likes or respects you, and is motivated to respond as you would like.

Why You Should Practice Diplomacy. The reason for practicing diplomacy in your letters is that it will encourage your readers to respond favorably to you and your requests or comments. The happier you make someone feel, the more that person will tend to like or admire you. The more favorable the impression that someone has of you, the more likely he or she is to try to work with you and get along with you. So diplomacy is a psychological tool that creates good relations and prevents or overcomes bad relations, which can only benefit everyone.

Emphasize the Positive. Everyone likes to receive a pleasing, flattering, attentive letter. But not everyone likes to write such a letter, particularly when the reader is unknown or disliked. Sometimes flattery is not even the right approach and may sound insincere. Being diplomatic in such cases may require more effort than normally would be necessary.

Whether or not you like a person, there is no reason not to focus on positive aspects of the relationship. If you were both elected to a committee, for example, you could emphasize the important, useful work that the committee is doing. Composing messages that emphasize the positive and eliminate the negative is part of the art of letter writing.

Revising Your Drafts. To be able to compose a diplomatic letter may mean that you have to set aside personal prejudices and hostilities, much the same as international diplomats do in foreign relations. It may mean that you have to write a first draft as you feel and then revise the letter, rephrasing anything that sounds cold and offensive. The process will be much easier, though, if you have tact and consideration in mind while you're preparing the first draft.

How to Make Pleasant Remarks. Since the opening of a letter sets the tone, and the concluding remarks leave the reader with a final impression, take advantage of those two places to say something pleasant. Here's a useful list of pleasing comments that you can refer to each time you write.

"It was good to hear from you."
"I appreciated your thoughtfulness in promptly sending the information I requested."
"Congratulations! It was wonderful to hear your news, and we want to wish you both much love and happiness."
"Thank you so much for all your help. I couldn't have managed without you."
"I sincerely appreciate your interest in this project. Many thanks."
"Please call me if you have any problems. We're eager to help you any way we can."
"I was very impressed with your suggestion to put the policy manuals on diskette. This type of creative thinking is what makes our company a success."

To develop other such comments, simply start with positive words, such as *thank you* and *appreciate*. Avoid negative words, such as *demand* and *wrong*. Skilled writers often begin and end their letters with a thoughtful or appreciative comment. But be careful not to overdo it. Section 24 has an example of a letter that is so gushy that it sounds insincere.

How to Handle Delicate Matters. The most difficult part of diplomacy is saying something potentially offensive in an acceptable way. Assume, for example, that you have to deny a request from a prospective customer and do it without losing the customer. An important objective should be to avoid saying "no, but thanks anyway," in a cold, abrupt manner.

Dear Mrs. Winters:

Thank you very much for letting us know about your interest in opening an account at B. C. Supplies.

As much as we would like to extend credit, we regretfully cannot do so at present. A review of your firm's credit report indicates occasional payment problems, and it is our policy in such cases to ship merchandise C.O.D. or by advance cash payment. However, if you would like to place orders on this basis for six months, we will be happy to consider your request again at that time.

We appreciate your thinking of B. C. Supplies and would welcome an opportunity to serve you. Please let us know if we can help in any other way.

Cordially,

An important part of diplomacy is stating a reason for your position honestly but tactfully, as the previous letter does. Follow this practice in personal correspondence too.

Dear Liz,

How I wish that I could accept your invitation to lunch on Monday, March 2. As much as I would love to see you, Liz, I'm sorry to say that I'll be stuck in the library all day. We're expanding, and several of us agreed to eat a sandwich at our desks and put in a little extra time.

I do hope we can meet another day. In the
meantime, thank you so much for asking.

Take care.

Love,

The one rule that applies to everything you say in correspondence is to put yourself in the reader's place before you
say it. Read your letter back before sending it and pretend
that someone else just sent it to you. Does it make you feel
good or bad or indifferent? If it puts a smile on your face—
even if it contains a rejection—you've succeeded in being a
diplomat.

28. APPLY THE FINE ART OF PERSUASION

Persuading someone to do something is an everyday exercise.
You may try to persuade your uncle to see a doctor or entice a
prospective customer to buy the product your company sells.
In this respect, many of your letters are "sales" letters, so the
question isn't whether you ever have occasion to use persuasive techniques; the question is how effectively you apply
them every day.

Specialists are usually retained to handle large sales
campaigns, major fund-raising drives, and other important
activities involving persuasive efforts. But everyone should
learn how to write persuasive letters for other personal and
professional purposes.

How to Create Letters That Persuade

A letter that persuades someone to do or think something
needs special attention. It can't be dashed off in a couple
minutes the way you might hastily compose a brief one- or

two-sentence routine inquiry. The following letter asking for donations, for example, should have received much more attention. In its present form, it's not likely to motivate the reader to get out his checkbook. Even if the reader does decide to contribute, the letter doesn't do anything to encourage him to give more than the requested minimum.

> Dear Fred:
>
> I'm handling our company's campaign this year for the working disabled. I'd like everyone to give $25 or more so we can exceed last year's donation of $7,500.
>
> Please send your gift as soon as possible, using the enclosed reply envelope. Thanks for your help.
>
> Regards,

The writer would have more luck if he sounded concerned and enthusiastic himself. If you sound bored and unconcerned in your letters, your readers may respond in the same way. Here's a different version that adds a little life to the ho-hum attitude of the first version.

> Dear Fred:
>
> Have you ever tried to climb very steep stairs with your arms so full that you couldn't hold onto the side rail? Or with a sprained ankle or a bum knee that made every step agonizingly painful?
>
> Physically challenged workers all over the country and those right here at Whitland Industries have to cope with a lot more than that--every minute of every day. That's why I'm so pleased to be this year's chair of our company's fund-raising campaign for The Working Disabled of America.

This year Whitland wants to surpass the previous year's goal of raising $7,500. The money will again be donated to The Working Disabled of America at its annual banquet in April. We can reach this goal if you and I and everyone else at Whitland will give $25 or more.

How about it, Fred--can I count on you to make a tax-deductible donation this year? Please send as much as you can, and make your check payable to The Working Disabled of America.

Use the enclosed envelope to send your gift today.

With thanks for your help and concern,

Effective Techniques. Here are examples of techniques that will help you to write persuasive letters.

- Say something to arouse the reader's curiosity or interest right away: "We have exciting news to tell you."
- Make statements that appeal to the reader's emotion or reason: "No one today can afford to lose his or her life savings—but it happens."
- State the merits of your argument clearly and in terms that relate to the reader: "This plan will accomplish the two things you most want: (1) It will put an end to long delays on your way to and from work, and (2) it will reduce the current accident rate on exit and entry ramps by as much as 50 percent."
- Offer the reader something: "Buy one bottle before the September 14 deadline, and you'll receive another full bottle of the same size absolutely <u>free</u>!"
- Select persuasive words that will enforce your message: *advantage, confidence, economical, free, great, guarantee, largest, new, powerful, proven, quality, quickly, results, successful, super, value.*
- Close by asking the reader to take a specific action: "Take advantage of this once-in-a-lifetime offer—mail the enclosed reply card today!"

The particular techniques you use depend on the type of persuasive letter you're writing. For example, you would take a personal I—you approach for a personal letter but would switch to a businesslike we—you approach for a business letter written on behalf of a company.

You would then follow the same principles that apply to any other type of letter: Be honest and sincere, and use language appropriate for the reader's background and level of comprehension. In a persuasive letter, though, don't hesitate to repeat main points for emphasis or add a postscript that refers again to the main point. This is one type of letter in which repetition is not only allowable but often desirable. For examples of undesirable repetition, see Section 37, and refer to other sections in this chapter for additional writing tips.

29. USE FAMILIAR, CONVERSATIONAL LANGUAGE

The Importance of Using Familiar Language

To avoid misunderstandings, it's important to use language that is familiar to both you and the reader in all correspondence. If a letter writer isn't familiar with certain terminology, he or she may misuse it. If the reader isn't familiar with it, he or she may not understand it. Although this advice sounds as though it should be obvious to anyone composing a letter, it isn't. Many letter writers regularly ignore it.

The next letter, for example, written by a banking representative to a customer, uses language that may be unfamiliar to the reader. The person had written to ask why the bank wouldn't let her use funds she deposited. This question in itself should have alerted the writer that the reader didn't understand the concept of a "hold" and might remain confused if the letter's language was too complex.

Dear Mrs. Lawson:

Thank you for asking about bank policy regarding funds availability on customer deposits.

The Expedited Funds Availability Act governs the time for which banking institutions may place a hold on customer deposits. Our bank is in compliance with the new regulations, which specify accessibility within three days on local checks and seven days on nonlocal checks. In the event that a hold is imposed on one of your checks, the bank is obligated to provide disclosure information to you at that time.

Please let us know if you have any additional questions.

Sincerely,

The writer could be more confident that the reader would understand if he used language more familiar to someone who apparently doesn't grasp the idea of "holds."

Dear Mrs. Lawson:

Thank you for asking about bank policy in placing a "hold" on a deposit you made.

Our bank must follow the rules of a law called the Expedited Funds Availability Act. This law tells us how long it may be necessary for you to wait before you can use the money from a check you deposit.

Sometimes when you deposit a check, it is necessary to wait a few days until the check "clears"--until the money from it is available for you to use. But the law states that when you deposit a local check, you will not have to wait more than three days before you can use the money. If you deposit a check that is not local, you will not have to wait more than seven days before you can use the money.

Our bank is required to follow these rules and therefore cannot "hold" the money on a check you deposit longer than the three-day or seven-day period. If a hold is placed on your deposit, the bank must explain these rules to you at the time you make the deposit. This is known as "disclosure."

If ever you do not understand why you cannot immediately use the money from one of your deposits, please ask for further explanation. We very much appreciate your concern and want to be certain that we have answered all your questions.

Sincerely,

The Importance of Using Conversational Language

Many people mistakenly believe that a letter has to be written in a straightforward, formal manner that is distinctly different from the tone and style used in everyday speech. But this approach usually leads to a cold, impersonal letter that repels rather than invites. Sometimes the letter writers who follow this path sound pompous or indifferent to the reader's needs. Skilled letter writers therefore use a relaxed, friendly, conversational tone in all general domestic correspondence.

Notice the difference in the next two letters. The first is stiff and cold, whereas the second is conversational and friendly.

My dear Mr. Bryant:

It was indeed thoughtful and generous of you to request my participation in the Community Pageant. It is with the deepest regret, therefore, that I must decline your kind invitation.

Please accept my good wishes for your success
in arranging the affair.

Yours truly,

Dear Mr. Bryant:

Thank you so much for asking me to
participate in the Community Pageant. How I
wish that I could join you, but unfortunately,
my monthly trip to the West Coast is scheduled
for the very week of the pageant.

Although I'm disappointed that I can't accept
your thoughtful invitation, I wish you much
success in arranging this year's festivities.

With best wishes,

Exceptions to the advice to use conversational language are
formal invitations, which are always written in formal
language (see Section 59 in Chapter 7), and international correspondence, which should be more formal than domestic
correspondence (see Chapter 6).

Colloquial Language. Conversational language should not
be confused with colloquial language. Although colloquial
language is conversational, it does not conform to all the
requirements of standard English and sometimes contains
slang, cliches, and other language that should be avoided.
Refer to Section 48 in Chapter 5 for more about the difference
between conversational and colloquial language.

30. BE CLEAR AND SPECIFIC

Fewer problems and misunderstandings will occur if you are
clear and specific in each letter you write. Writing letters that
are clear and specific, however, usually takes more time and
involves more work than writing letters that are vague and

general. To an overworked person for whom each day is already too short, it sometimes doesn't seem worth the time and effort. But it is.

Taking time to be clear and specific should be mandatory—unless you have a special reason why you need to be vague and general. (Perhaps you don't want to make a commitment, or mention a specific individual, reveal the exact details about something, or describe something too narrowly.) But being deliberately vague and general is an exception to the rule and should not be used as justification for abandoning the rule.

Writing Letters That Are Clear and Specific

Avoid Abstract, General Terms. If you want your letters to shine with clarity, avoid abstract, general expressions. Take your next draft and underline expressions that seem vague and general. For each underlined expression, find a concrete substitute.

Here are examples of specific terms that could be substituted for general expressions.

General Expression	Specific Term
building	city hall, grade school, supermarket
color	red, green, blue
impeccable	accurate, clean, neat
misfortune	death in the family, car accident, storm damage
pay	commission, honorarium, salary
tools	scissors, ruler, knife
unfit	unhealthy, untrained, incapable
vehicle	car, boat, truck
work	word processing, telecommunications, accounting

Most of the time, you'll help your readers by choosing a specific term over a general term. But the following letter writer fails to heed that advice.

Dear Ruth,

I've been thinking more and more about the comments Beth made at the last PTA meeting. I think she's right, don't you? Why don't we get together in a couple weeks and talk about it some more. We might even get people to sign something supporting our idea.

Call me if you want to get things moving.

Best,

Although Ruth was presumably at the same PTA meeting, should the writer be assuming that Ruth will remember what Beth said? What time and day does the writer want to meet? What exactly does the writer mean by "get things moving"?

Letter writers sometimes incorrectly assume that readers know what they mean even when they don't say it. In the preceding example, the writer should have been clearer and more specific about everything, even if she believed that Ruth knew precisely what she was talking about. For example:

Dear Ruth,

I've been thinking more and more about Beth's suggestion at the August 6 PTA meeting to form a Community Awareness Committee. I think that's a good idea, don't you?

Why don't you, Beth, and I get together on Saturday, August 16, at 2 o'clock at my house to talk about it? We might be able to draw up a petition that the neighbors could sign to let the school board know that everyone supports the idea of a new committee.

Call me if you'd like to meet with Beth and me to discuss creating a petition and other steps we might take to persuade the school board that we need this committee.

Best,

Being clear and specific means not only using more concrete terms but also including enough information to be certain that the reader understands your suggestions and how you want the reader to respond. It means using good paragraphing and other composition techniques to make a letter easy to read. It means giving all necessary details, such as the "who, what, where, when, and why" approach used by newspaper reporters.

Who, What, Where, When, Why. In the second version of the letter to Ruth, the writer answers the major questions.

Question	Answer
who	the writer, Ruth, Beth
what	have an informal meeting
where	the writer's house
when	Saturday, August 16, 2 o'clock
why	discuss Beth's suggestion to create a Community Awareness Committee and create a petition to show the school board that the idea of a new committee has community support

Reread the next letter you write and see whether it passes the "who, what, where, when, and why" test. Not all messages, however, require an answer to each question. A sympathy message, for example, wouldn't fit that mold. But letters that discuss an event, idea, or action should answer most or all of the questions to make the message clear and specific to the reader.

31. CHOOSE WORDS CAREFULLY TO AVOID MISUNDERSTANDINGS

Using the wrong words in your letters can get you into trouble. This happens when you pick a wrong word that is frequently misused, is commonly confused with a similar term, or sounds like but is not spelled like the word you really want to use (homophone).

Choosing the Right Word

Choosing the right word means selecting a word that means precisely what you want to express. Even skilled letter writers sometimes use the wrong word. This often happens because they are composing a message too quickly or because they don't spend enough time reviewing and proofreading the message before sending it.

Confusables. Just as a typist may repeatedly press the wrong key and create a typo, a letter writer may repeatedly misuse certain words, for example, using *infer* instead of *imply*. (See Section 49 in Chapter 6 for examples of commonly confused terms.) Foreign readers, who often translate everything literally, could gain the wrong impression from such a mistake. (Refer to Chapter 6 for more about word choice in international correspondence.) Domestic readers, too, might be confused; at the very least they might think the letter writer is careless or ignorant.

Notice how using *liable* for *likely* creates an unintended meaning in this letter.

Dear Bob:

Yes, the new program has been initiated. Midwest Equipment Exporters is now marketing the gears in three European countries and, considering the program directive, is liable to begin selling in Japan.

I'm enclosing a copy of the revised program summary. It will explain the regional strategy, but let me know if you have any questions.

Best regards,

According to the letter writer, the company "is legally responsible" (*is liable*) for marketing in Japan. But the writer really meant the company "just might" (*is likely to*) sell in Japan. The reader may or may not understand this; a foreign reader probably would not.

Homophones. Words that sound alike but have different meanings are *homophones*. (See Section 49 in Chapter 6 for examples.) In the next letter, the writer has confused *eluded* (evaded) with *alluded* (referred indirectly).

Dear Shana,

Thank you so much for the copy of Dave's article. I was disappointed, however, that he eluded to the problem of the environment but didn't really address it. Perhaps space was limited, and he couldn't discuss it in depth. Otherwise, I thought he made some useful points.

I enjoyed seeing his work and appreciate your thoughtfulness in sending me a copy.

Best wishes,

As in all other cases of incorrect word choice, the letter writer here appears either careless or ignorant.

Incorrect Definitions. Another type of error occurs when a letter writer doesn't know the correct definition of a word. For example, a writer may mistakenly believe that *exacerbating* means improving something when it really means making something more violent or severe. Such mistakes make a writer appear ignorant, and all effort should be made to avoid this type of error. Anyone who feels uneasy about using certain terms in a letter should either pick a more familiar term or consult a dictionary before the letter is mailed.

The next section points out the benefits of using short, simple words in your letters.

32. USE SHORT, SIMPLE WORDS AND SENTENCES

Conversation versus Correspondence

If more letter writers wrote the way they talked, the subject of Section 29, they would regularly use short, simple words and sentences. No one would say this in ordinary conversation:

> "I shall endeavor to determine the causative factors in declining sales this quarter."

More likely, someone would say this.

> "I'll try to find out why sales are down this quarter."

Letters written in a conversational tone are more easily read and understood.

How to Simplify Your Messages

Since people are more likely to use simple, readily understandable language in speech, any effort to write the way you talk will help. If that doesn't work, you should reread your letters and substitute short, simple words and sentences for any longer, more complex versions that you find.

Section 51 in Chapter 6 explains how to use short words, sentences, and paragraphs to make your international messages easier to translate. All of the tips in that section can be applied to domestic messages. Although English-speaking readers may be able to figure out what you mean, most of them won't have the time or energy to linger over complex, cumbersome, pretentious prose. Section 44 in Chapter 5 explains how to avoid big, pretentious words and phrases in your letters.

Guidelines. Refer to the examples in Section 51 of Chapter 6 and Section 44 of Chapter 5 and apply these guidelines.

- When you have a choice, select a word with only one or two syllables rather than one with several syllables (*disperse/disseminate*).
- If many words have prefixes (*semiautomatic*) or suffixes (*management*), recast some sentences to eliminate a few of them.
- Avoid using a long, rambling sentence that constitutes a paragraph in itself. Try breaking it up into two or three shorter sentences.
- Although individual situations vary, the more words a sentence has, the harder it is to read and comprehend. Sentences in international correspondence should generally not range beyond ten to fifteen words.
- Avoid pompous words and phrases (*commence, bona fide*).
- Use short paragraphs, and especially, try to keep the first paragraph of a letter very short.
- Use displayed lists, tables, and other easy-to-follow formats to simplify a long series of items or complex factual information. Anything that breaks up information into short, compact bits is easier to follow and remember.

In your effort to use short, simple words and sentences, keep in mind the following exceptions.

- Using short, simple words and sentences should not be confused with using simple concepts; rather, a simple presentation should be used to make complex concepts easier to comprehend.
- Even though short words are usually simpler than long words, be careful not to use short words that are less familiar to certain readers than a longer substitute (*spae/foretell*).
- Although it's important to use short, simple words and sentences whenever possible, it's also important to vary word and sentence length to avoid monotony.

Long, complex words, sentences, and paragraphs are usually more confusing and therefore detract from the clarity of a message. Simplicity will therefore contribute to another goal in letter writing—being clear and specific, the subject of Section 30.

33. USE THE ACTIVE VOICE

Active and Passive Voices

The *active voice* is a grammatical term indicating that the subject of a verb is performing the action: "He signed the contract." In that sentence it's obvious that *he*, the subject, performed the action of signing the contract.

If the subject had been acted upon, the sentence would be in the *passive voice*: "The contract was signed by him." In this case the *contract*, the subject, is being acted upon; it isn't performing any action.

Why Letter Writers Prefer the Active Voice

Most letter writers prefer the active voice because it's more direct and more powerful, and it adds life to a letter. The passive voice is considered less direct and weaker. Notice the difference in the next two letters. The first uses the passive voice, and the second uses the active voice.

Dear Mr. Whittaker:

In reply to your letter of December 19 concerning your order of December 1, it is expected that a shipping date of January 10 will be possible.

Merchandise is shipped by ground transportation unless another preference has been requested. If this is not satisfactory, please let us know.

Your business is very much appreciated, and we hope to serve you again.

Sincerely,

Dear Mr. Whittaker:

Thank you for asking about the shipping date of your December 1 order. We expect to ship your order on January 10.

We usually ship merchandise by ground transportation unless a customer has another preference. If this method is not satisfactory, please let us know.

We appreciate your business, Mr. Whittaker, and hope to serve you again.

Sincerely,

Not only is the second version using the active voice more direct and stronger, but it is also friendlier. The passive voice seems to put more distance between the letter writer and the reader. It gives the impression that the letter writer prefers not to be involved or closely associated with the reader.

When the Passive Voice Is Useful

Although letter writers prefer the active voice most of the time, the passive voice can be helpful if you want to be less committal or less direct and forceful. In the next example, the first letter using the active voice is a little too bold and personally critical. The second version uses the passive voice to make the comments more diplomatic.

Dear Herm:

I finished reading your report last night and want to thank you for all the work you put into it. I have only two comments.

1. You mentioned postal mail and private-transport delivery on page 2 but did not discuss the important subject of electronic mail.

2. You made one typo on page 11--<u>them</u> for <u>the</u>.

If you could check those two items before we make additional copies, I'd appreciate it, Herm. Thanks for a good job!

Regards,

Dear Herm:

I finished reading your report last night and want to thank you for all the work you put into it. I have only two comments.

1. Page 2: Postal and private mail are mentioned, but the important subject of electronic mail is not discussed.

2. Page 11: A typo was found--<u>them</u> for <u>the</u>.

If you could check those two items before we make additional copies, I'd appreciate it, Herm. Thanks for a good job!

Regards,

Sentences That Require the Passive Voice. Occasionally, the passive voice not only is desirable but also may be the only choice: "Two hundred rioters were arrested in Bingham City last year." You couldn't logically say that "Bingham City arrested two hundred rioters last year." So the passive voice must be used unless you can add more to the sentence to make it possible to switch to an active voice: "The *police* arrested two hundred rioters in Bingham City last year."

34. USE ADJECTIVES AND ADVERBS SPARINGLY

Some adjectives will always be necessary to make your statements clear and precise or to add enough color and emotion to a comment to make your words come to life. But letter writers need to be careful not to use unnecessary adjectives and adverbs.

Using Adjectives

An *adjective* is a part of speech that modifies, describes, or limits a noun or pronoun: "A *large* company has a *competitive* advantage." Both of those adjectives immediately precede the nouns they modify. A *predicate adjective* appears after the noun and is connected to it by a linking verb: "The company is *large*."

When an Adjective Is Necessary. If a sentence isn't clear or complete without a certain adjective, or if you can't create the mood or impression you want without it, the adjective is necessary. In the next letter the italicized adjectives contribute to the clarity of the writer's comments.

Dear Mrs. Jiani:

Thank you for letting us know that the *boysenberry* squares you received did not have *chocolate-covered* walnuts on them as advertised. Apparently, catalog number B-SQ12 was inadvertently substituted for BC-SQ12 when your order was filled.

We are sending you the *correct* item today by United Parcel Service. It should reach you by Friday, June 23. We will also ask the driver to pick up the *incorrect* shipment when he delivers the *replacement* order to your address.

Please accept our apologies for the confusion. We appreciate your order and hope that you will soon be enjoying our *prizewinning, boysenberry* squares coated with *delectable, chocolate-covered* walnuts.

Cordially,

The adjectives in the first paragraph identify the order. The customer may have ordered other squares besides boysenberry squares, so mentioning *boysenberry* is necessary. Other pastries may have caramel-covered walnuts or something else, so the compound adjective *chocolate-covered* clarifies that part of the order.

The second paragraph would sound too vague without the adjectives *correct, incorrect,* and *replacement*

Finally, the third paragraph again identifies the squares as boysenberry and the walnuts as chocolate covered. The adjectives *delectable* and *prizewinning* are included as the writer's way of reminding the customer that these squares are very special and well worth waiting for.

When an Adjective Is Not Necessary. Some letter writers embellish their messages too much. It isn't necessary for clarity and may even detract from the essence of a message by cluttering the sentences with an excess of modifiers. By omitting the italicized adjectives in this letter, the message would be stronger.

Dear Michelle,

I still can't believe I tipped over that *big, tall,* full jug of *lemon-fresh* bleach on your bathroom carpet. Although you kindly insisted that the stain was minor, it was obvious to me, and I sincerely apologize.

Could I send a *good, top-notch,* professional cleaner out to work on it? I didn't think of it at the time, but a professional may have some means of making the *terrible, awful* discoloration less noticeable.

I'm hoping you'll let me do this or make it up to you in some other way--and I promise not to be so clumsy in the future.

Love,

The italicized adjectives add nothing useful and create the impression that the writer tends to be excessive and exaggerate everything.

Using Adverbs

An *adverb* is a part of speech that modifies, describes, qualifies, or limits a verb, verbal (gerund, participle, infinitive), adjective, or another adverb: "The unemployment rate is *slowly* declining." The adverb *slowly* modifies the adjective *declining.* Adverbs often answer the questions "where," "how," "when," or "to what extent." The adverb *too* in the next sentence modifies another adverb (*well*) and tells us "how" well: "The sales clerk knew that feeling all *too* well."

When an Adverb Is Necessary. As with an adjective, if a sentence isn't clear or complete without a certain adverb, or if you can't create the mood or impression you want without it, the adverb is necessary. In the next letter, the italicized adverb *very much* in the first paragraph helps to set the friendly tone the writer wants to convey. In the next paragraph, *recently* is necessary for clarity.

> Dear Mr. Orville:
>
> Did you forget something? I thought I'd remind you that your payment of $165.99 to The Country Store will be *very much* appreciated.
>
> If your check was *recently* mailed, please disregard this letter and accept our thanks. But if you haven't sent your payment yet, won't you take a moment to mail it today?
>
> Cordially,

When an Adverb Is Not Necessary. When an adverb isn't needed for clarity or to create a desired tone, it tends to clutter a sentence as much as an unnecessary adjective does. This letter would be strengthened if the italicized adverbs were omitted.

> Dear Ms. Bowes:
>
> We want to let you know that because of a *strangely* long delay from our supplier we have had to back-order the copy paper you requested. However, we will ship your order as soon as a new supply is *clearly* available to our warehouse.
>
> Thank you for your *patiently* thoughtful cooperation. We apologize for the delay and hope it will not *completely* inconvenience you.
>
> Sincerely,

Most of the overuse of adverbs involves modifiers like this: *absolutely* necessary policy, *clearly* able teacher, *perfectly* clear instructions, and *richly* deserved award. In most cases, you could simply omit such adverbs. If you wanted to say more or provide greater emphasis, however, you could recast the entire sentence so that it isn't necessary to use an adverbial expression that sounds like a cliche: "The instructions are clear and easy to read."

For more information about adjectives and adverbs, as well as other parts of speech, refer to a recent edition of a book of grammar, such as *The Elements of Grammar* (Macmillan).

35. GET TO THE POINT IN YOUR OPENING

Writing Successful Letter Openings

If you want to get the reader's attention, keep your letter opening short and get right to the point. Long, rambling openings force a reader to wait to find out what you want.

You can see how easy it might be to lose someone's attention in the next example.

Dear Mr. Wyckoff:

On September 11 we asked for a part-time computer operator for our Word Processing Department. You recommended Lora Jane Baxter and sent us a summary of her skills and experience. The information indicated that she had worked in an operator capacity previously and had just completed two computer courses at Norville Junior College.

Lora Jane has been with us about three weeks, working twenty hours a week. We have appreciated her pleasant manner, businesslike appearance, and steady work habits. But unfortunately, her typing speed has not reached the rate we would like. Although I'm certain that her speed will eventually improve as her experience increases, we are unable to wait for the benefits of additional work experience. Rather, we are in immediate need of an operator with a higher typing speed. Therefore, we would like to have a replacement for Lora Jane ready by October 12.

Please telephone me at 555-1400 to discuss the qualifications of a possible replacement for Lora Jane. Thanks very much.

Sincerely,

No one wants to wait until almost the end of a letter to find out what the writer is trying to say. Instead, as the next letter illustrates, a writer should get to the point in the first paragraph or even the first sentence—and then make any other pertinent points in additional paragraphs.

Dear Mr. Wyckoff:

We would like to request a replacement for Lora Jane Baxter, the part-time computer operator sent to us from your agency on September 11. I'm sorry to let you know that her typing speed is too slow for our needs.

The information you had sent us about Lora Jane's experience indicated that she had previously worked as a computer operator and had completed two computer courses at Norville Junior College. Although this background is apparently insufficient for our needs, we want to commend Lora Jane for her pleasant manner, businesslike appearance, and steady work habits.

Since we are in immediate need of an experienced operator with a higher typing speed, we would appreciate having a replacement ready to begin by October 12.

Please telephone me at 555-1400 to discuss the qualifications of a possible replacement for Lora Jane. Thanks very much.

Sincerely,

Techniques for Better Letter Openings

The advice to get to the point and keep the opening of a letter short are essential for successful letter openings. Using other techniques will make an opening even better. For example:

- Use the reader's name in the first paragraph or first sentence (essential with a simplified format, as described in Section 55 of Chapter 7): "Thank you for asking about our international designs for polo shirts, Ms. Brady."
- Begin by saying something pleasant: "I was impressed with your detailed and interesting analysis, Don."

- Refer to something of mutual interest: "You'll be happy to learn that the library reorganization we recommended has been endorsed by all department heads."
- Use the "who," "what," "where," "when," and "why" approach recommended in Section 30: "We're happy to let you know that as of April 1 [*when*] Surelite Manufacturing [*who*] will expand its on-site [*where*] training program [*what*] to include retraining of employees whose jobs are being eliminated [*why*]."
- Use attention-grabbing techniques, such as stating an unusual fact, asking a question, or referring to a famous person: "Francis Bacon once said that 'knowledge is power.' If you agree, we'd like to tell you about an amazing new publication."

Refer to Section 40 for guidelines on writing successful closings.

36. EMPHASIZE THE KEY POINTS OF YOUR MESSAGE

Some letters make only one point. A thank you note, for example, should only express appreciation for something received. Other types of letters might make two or more points. Those letters are more difficult to write.

Pinpointing Main Ideas

Sometimes it's easy to confuse the key points of a letter with the supporting points. You may provide numerous facts and figures in a letter, but usually, most of such information enhances, supports, or otherwise sells the key points.

Assume that your alumni association is selling halogen desk lamps that are part high tech and part modern sculpture. The sales from these sculpture-lamps will provide income for your college to be used to improve the programs and fill other important needs. The lamps, in a brass design, will rotate 360 degrees and will stand 18 inches high. How many *key points* are in that description. Two main points stand out: (1) The association is selling sculpture-lamps, and (2) the income will be used to benefit the college. Everything else is supporting material.

Techniques for Highlighting Key Points. After you have identified your main points, you can highlight them in various ways.

- Briefly identify the key points in your opening paragraph.
- Mention one key point in the lead sentence of each succeeding paragraph.
- In a sales or direct-mail letter, present the lead sentences identifying the key points in bold face or underline them.
- Precede the paragraphs discussing the key points with a bold-face subheading.
- Summarize an important point in a postscript.

Techniques for Presenting Supporting Material. The facts and figures that support your key points should be presented in a way that makes their supporting status clear. Through appropriate organization of sentences and paragraphs or through various formatting techniques, you can alert the reader that these facts and figures are secondary to the main ideas.

- Place the sentences with supporting information after the lead (key-point) sentences.
- Itemize numerous facts or figures as an indented list.
- Highlight listed items with bullets or another mark.

Organizing Key Points and Supporting Material

If your letter will be brief and will contain only one or two main points, you may be able to organize the information mentally. But some people prefer to write a rough draft and then revise it as needed to improve the arrangement of main and supporting points. Others like to work from an outline, particularly if extensive information is involved. Refer to Section 19 in Chapter 3 and Section 20 in this chapter for more about outlining a detailed letter.

Composing the Message

Whether you work from notes, an outline, or neither, follow the guidelines just given for highlighting key points and presenting supporting material.

Dear Alumni and Friends:

I'm pleased to announce that the Alumni Association of Alton College has commissioned the fine craftspeople at Modern Art for Living to produce an exquisite sculpture-lamp especially for alumni and friends. Income from the sales of this beautiful lamp will provide support for the college's most pressing needs this year.

<u>This exciting desk sculpture-lamp is available now from the Alumni Association at Alton College</u>. As pictured on the enclosed order blank, the sculpture-lamp will include all of these features--and more.

- High-tech desk lamp for house or office
- Design in modern brass
- 360-degree rotation
- 18 inches high
- Generous 6-foot cord
- Long-life, 50-watt halogen bulb

This combination lamp and work of art is available for only $98.99 <u>including</u> shipping and handling.

<u>As part of the college's annual fund-raising effort, income from sales will be applied toward the most pressing programs and other greatest needs</u>. Your purchase, for example, will directly help the college modernize some of its aging

facilities and expand programs in important new areas, such as computers and international trade. As Alton College strengthens its programs and facilities, students both now and in the future will benefit.

Please consider ordering a modern sculpture-lamp for your home or office and at the same time help Alton College move toward the twenty-first century. I know you'll cherish this wonderful work of art.

Sincerely,

Robert Marshall

P.S. Use the enclosed order form to send your check today.

The same procedure for emphasizing key points that was applied in this sales letter can be used in any other type of letter.

37. Avoid Unnecessary Repetition

Everyone would agree that it's best to avoid *unnecessary* repetition in correspondence. The question is, what is necessary and what is unnecessary?

When Repetition Is Necessary or Useful

If you find repetition in your letters, ask yourself the following questions.

- Does the repetition help to underscore an important point?
- Does the repetition serve as a reminder to readers to respond in a specific way?

- Is the repetition necessary to create a desired stylistic or rhythmic effect?
- Is the repetition part of a summary or concluding paragraph in your letter?

Professional letter writers intentionally use repetition with success. Notice how repetition, shown in italics, is used intentionally in the next letter to implant certain words and ideas in the reader's mind.

Dear Mr. Cramwell:

POLICY 22 JMZ 1278349

We're happy that the *JMZ automobile insurance program*, the *program of choice* for millions of Americans, has also been the *program of choice* for you this year. Since your first year of coverage has almost ended, however, we'd like to take this opportunity to review your file with you.

Our records show your name and address as listed at the top of this letter. *Our records* also *show* that you filed one claim during the past year.

DRIVER: Cramwell, Jeffrey L.
INCIDENT DATE: March 24, 1994
DESCRIPTION: Accident

If you have any questions about your policy, please call us toll-free at 1-800-555-2525. One of our service representatives will be happy to help you.

We look forward to making the *JMZ automobile insurance program* your *program* for another year.

Cordially,

Skilled letter writers also use other kinds of repetition, such as repeating the style or form of saying something.

"The time is past for dreaming. The time is past for complaining. The time is past for assuming that someone else will make things better. Yes, the time is past for all of that. But the time is here—today—for all of us to send our collective message to the City Council. That message is clear: We demand more accountability of elected officials to the citizens of Cherryville."

When Repetition Is Unnecessary. A fine line exists between effective repetition and overkill. If you have any doubts about whether you're carrying the technique too far, avoid it. Especially, look for repetition that serves no stylistic or emphatic purpose in your letters. The italicized words in the following examples unnecessarily repeat or emphasize the thought that is adequately expressed by the rest of the words.

"My work is now nearly complete *at this time.*"
"I'll look forward to seeing you in my office at 2 p.m. Friday *afternoon.*"
"The *close* proximity of the waterway should help us reduce transportation costs."
"Our eastern office is in *the state of* New Jersey."

The next section on wordiness has additional tips on eliminating unnecessary words and expressions.

38. GUARD AGAINST WORDINESS

The Pros and Cons of Word Economy

Most communications instructors would urge you to practice word economy. They believe that you should use only essential words and should not use three or four words when one or two words would accomplish the same thing.

Word economy is usually good advice, provided you don't trim so much fat from your messages that they sound curt and choppy. Transition words, for example, such as *however,* may not be crucial to an understanding of your message. But they make one sentence or paragraph flow smoothly into another and thus serve a useful purpose. Cutting so much that your message becomes abrupt and awkward would be contrary to the advice to be friendly and conversational. See Section 29.

Letter writers need to use common sense in deciding whether certain words serve a useful purpose or are merely superfluous. Because of the special tone and quality that correspondence requires, you might at times decide against the strictest forms of word economy. Even if you can clearly state something in ten words, for example, you should not hesitate to use twelve or fourteen words if doing so will help you achieve a friendlier or more persuasive tone.

Practicing Word Economy

Cutting Out the Clutter. Many extra words serve no useful purpose. They don't contribute to a smooth, conversational flow and don't make your letters any friendlier or more convincing. They only clutter a message and slow up the reader. The italicized words in the following sentences are examples of clutter.

> "*Your attention is directed to* the enclosed instruction sheet, *which* lists the proper steps for trouble-free operation."
> "The check is attached *hereto.*"
> "*This is to advise you that* we expect to ship your merchandise on November 6."

Reducing Lengthy Passages. Watch for lengthy passages in your letters that could be restated in fewer words. In the next example, the first letter has superfluous words and more detail than the reader needs. The second version cuts the original letter's more than 150 words to about 90 words.

Dear Ms. Schurter:

Referring to your recent question as to whether the Utility Rating Commission has reached a decision about revising its rating system, it has decided to delay revision of the present system until next year.

The Utility Rating Commission believes that there are many desirable changes that could be made in the present utility rating system in order to make it more efficient and more functional than it now is, but the commission is of the opinion that further modification in the present system during the current year would require retraining of staff and other administrative expense that might cause the commission to exceed its budget, and hence the commission believes that revision of the rating system should be postponed until next year when anticipated expenses can be built into the operating budget.

If you have any additional questions, Ms. Schurter, please let me know. We appreciate your interest in the rating system of the Utility Rating Commission.

Sincerely,

Dear Ms. Schurter:

Thank you for asking about a revision in the Utility Rating Commission's rating system.

The commission has decided to delay revision of its rating system until next year. Although it believes that the system can and should be improved, as you recommended, no provisions were made in this year's budget for the cost of a revision. But the commission expects to include the necessary funding in next year's budget.

If you have any additional questions, Ms.
Schurter, please let me know. We appreciate
your interest in the commission's utility rating
system.

Sincerely,

Editing Wordy Expressions. As you review the drafts of
your letters, look not only for unnecessarily detailed passages
but also wordy expressions. Often expressions of three to six
words can be reduced to one or two words. Here are some
examples.

Wordy Expression	Substitution
a great deal of	much
a number of	about
along the line of	like
as regards	for, about
at a later date	later
at a time when	when
at the present writing	now
due to the fact that	because
if at all possible	if possible
in order to	to
in the course of	during
in the majority of cases	usually
in the opinion of this writer	in my opinion, I believe
notwithstanding the fact that	although
the foregoing	the, this, that, these, those

Redundancies such as *final conclusion* sound foolish and are
never acceptable, but letter writers should not cut so many
extra words that a letter becomes a mere skeleton. Variety is
also an important ingredient in letter writing, and a professional writer knows when to turn to a longer expression, such
as *in favor of* instead of *for* or *to*, to break the monotony and

choppiness of passages that have numerous short forms. Knowing how to strike the right balance between word economy and smooth, interesting composition is something that comes with practice. Until then, if you have any doubts, opt for word economy over wordiness.

39. CREATE LOGICAL PARAGRAPHS

Determining the Size of Paragraphs

Letter writers should observe two important rules about paragraphing in correspondence: Use relatively short paragraphs, and make the first paragraph especially short.

Paragraphing in correspondence is different from paragraphing in other forms of publication, such as articles and books. Although long, cumbersome paragraphs would be questionable anywhere, they are especially uninviting in letters. An important objective in composing letters is to help the reader move through the letter quickly and easily while also encouraging the reader to reach a certain conclusion or take some desired action. Short paragraphs are essential for rapid reading and immediate comprehension.

Dividing the Text into Logical Paragraphs

Simplifying the Text. Because short paragraphs are so important in correspondence, you may not follow the traditional rule of one thought-one paragraph. If your one thought involves a lot of detail, you may use more than one paragraph to expand on a single idea. Or you may simplify a long, one-thought paragraph by extracting items in a series and writing them in list fashion. If the paragraph contains a long quotation or a special example, you may decide to write such material indented from the rest of the paragraph.

Use any clear, easy-to-follow formatting device that you like to simplify long paragraphs. For example:

TO: Bill McPhearson
FROM: Dan Fries

INTERVENTION CLAUSE FOR PUBLIC NOTICE

Here's a copy of our public notice about the proposed tariffs and service areas. I'd appreciate it if you would review the notice and let me know if the following legal statement about intervention is correct.

Any person having a direct and substantial interest and entitled by law to intervene will be permitted to do so. Those who want to intervene must file a written motion with the Regulatory Agency and send a copy to all parties of record. This motion must contain:

1. The name, address, and telephone of the intervenor

2. A short statement of the intervenor's interest in the proceedings

3. A statement certifying that a copy of the motion to intervene has been mailed to all parties of record

Those who do not intervene will receive no further notice of the proceedings unless notice is requested.

You can call me at extension 2694 with your comments, Bill. Many thanks.

Order of Paragraphs. The order in which you place the paragraphs in a letter depends on the key points you include. Section 36 discusses the matter of emphasizing key points in a message. Usually, the priority of key points determines in what order they should be mentioned. Often one point must be mentioned before another for the second one to make sense. If all major points are equally important and one need not precede another for clarity, the order may be unimportant.

Creating an outline to guide your composition is very helpful in determining the order of paragraphs. Follow the suggestions in Section 19 in Chapter 3.

In the previous letter about intervention requirements, the writer opens with a paragraph asking the reader to review a legal statement in his company's public notice. The second paragraph quotes the legal statement. Since it's a long, complex paragraph, the writer used both a blocked quotation and a list within the quotation to simplify the format. The third and final paragraph asks the reader to call with comments about the statement.

Readers should feel that, as they move from one paragraph to another, they are logically progressing from beginning to end or from introduction to conclusion. A reader should never have to skip back and forth to understand the message.

Construction of Paragraphs

Each paragraph should begin with a topic sentence that introduces the key point to be discussed in that paragraph. If you write from an outline, the topic sentence will be based on a key point on the outline. The opening sentence focuses the reader's attention on the key point to be discussed, and the sentences that follow support the key topic with facts, figures, and other details. Occasionally, the key point is written last, as a summary sentence, and sometimes a paragraph has both a key-point opening sentence and a key-point closing summary sentence.

The previous letter uses the most common construction—a key-point opening sentence that introduces the legal matter of intervention in public proceedings: "Any person having a direct and substantial interest and entitled by law to intervene will be permitted to do so." The remaining sentences provide the details—how to intervene by motion and what the motion must contain. This simple arrangement—an opening key-point sentence followed by supporting sentences with details—is the clearest and easiest arrangement for a reader to follow.

40. WRITE AN EFFECTIVE CLOSING

The closing paragraph in the body of a letter, not to be confused with the complimentary close, is just as important as the opening paragraph. It's especially important if you want the reader to take some action based on what you said in the previous paragraphs.

Writing Successful Letter Closings

Techniques for Better Endings. The principal objective of the closing is to bring the discussion to a conclusion and to make your final request. Here are some of the standard techniques used in writing effective ending paragraphs.

- Make the final paragraph brief and to the point: "I'll be happy to answer any other questions you have, Ms. Donatelli. You can reach me at 555-1623."
- Be courteous in your final remarks so that the reader will leave the letter with a favorable impression of you: "It's always wonderful to see you, Paul, and I'm looking forward to your next visit."
- If you want the reader to do something, suggest only one action; don't give the reader alternatives from which to choose: "Your copy of this booklet is waiting for you. Just O.K. and mail the enclosed card today."
- Do not reveal a lack of confidence in how the reader will respond to something you want; avoid doubtful words, such as *if*, and negative words, such as *can't*: "We're looking forward to receiving your outline."
- Avoid old-fashioned, stilted phrases ("May we have the pleasure of serving you?"): "We'll be happy to help you at any time. Just give us a call."
- Use dated action when you want something from the reader: "Please let me know your decision by December 1."
- Make the action requested of the reader as easy as possible: "Use the enclosed postage-paid reply card to reserve your copies today."

- Use positive, enticing words: "Our representative, John Ferris, someone I'm sure you'll enjoy, will call you next week to set up an appointment."
- Summarize a long, complex letter in the last sentence or two: "We appreciate your support of the Holliman Nature Center. The preservation of the center and its nature walk will enhance the quality of life for everyone in Holliman and the entire state."

When You Have Nothing More to Say. Often a letter writer has very little to say at the end of the letter. It's important not to begin a new topic at the end or resort to a cliche ending ("It was a pleasure to serve you"). If you have nothing to say, just stop writing. Usually, however, you can at least add a "thank you" or other very brief, polite remark. For example:

Dear Leslie Altman:

We recently mailed a new telephone calling card to your address shown above.

Did you receive it? If not, please call 1-800-555-6351 immediately. Our customer service representatives are available to assist you twenty-four hours a day, seven days a week.

If you have already received your new calling card, there is no need to call. But please remember to sign your card and place it in your wallet or purse where it will be ready to use. At the same time, please destroy your old card, which is no longer valid.

Thank you, and enjoy using your new calling card.

Sincerely,

Refer to Section 35 for techniques used in writing effective letter openings.

41. EDIT YOUR MESSAGE

Correcting Your Drafts

Unless you always do everything perfectly the first time around, you'll want to correct and polish your drafts before preparing the final copy for conventional mail or electronic transmission. Computers make this task especially easy, since you can type in corrections and change the format without having to retype the entire message yourself.

How to Edit. Most letter writers type or print out a copy of their draft and then use a pencil to cross out words, add new words, move words around, mark changes in formatting, and generally make everything sound and look better. If you're typing your own message, mark up your drafts any way that is clear to you. But if a secretary or someone else types your revised draft, write clearly so that the person won't misunderstand something and have to type it all over again.

Using a Checklist

If your messages tend to be long and complex, you may want to devise a checklist of the elements of correspondence that you want to examine before sending your message. Chapter 1 has two such checklists. One checklist (Section 3) has examples of questions to ask yourself when you review your work. Another checklist (Section 7) has questions to ask in evaluating form letters.

For general use, make a list of all aspects of correspondence that you need to remember to check each time you finish a draft. For example, have I used a proper format? Have I shown tact and diplomacy? Is my capitalization consistent? Are my topics and subtopics arranged in a logical order? Refer to the index and table of contents in this book for further ideas as you develop your checklist.

Look for topics that apply to the type of correspondence you write. If you write only personal, handwritten letters, you don't need to be concerned about choosing one of the standard business formats (see Section 55 in Chapter 7). If you never write international correspondence, you don't need to be concerned about statements that might offend someone in another country (see Section 53 in Chapter 6).

Most of the elements of correspondence described in this book apply to all types of messages—personal, social, and business. After it becomes a habit to check whether you handled each element properly, you may no longer need to use a formal checklist. By then, the procedure will be automatic.

5

Language to Avoid

42. AVOID EXCESSIVE USE OF BUSINESS JARGON

Business Jargon

If you look in a dictionary, you'll see several definitions of *jargon*, most of them indicating a specialized language or dialect unfamiliar or unintelligible to outsiders. *Business jargon* refers to a technical language or characteristic idiom used in a particular industry, profession, or group.

Excessive Use. Although letter writers who use jargon sometimes argue convincingly that business jargon is necessary for communication among members in a particular industry, profession, or group, it is considered undesirable when used outside the specialized activity. If you talk to a computer user about *accessing* the files or a database, for example, that's fine. But when you write to your Aunt Milli about *accessing* the refrigerator for a jar of jelly, that's going too far. The use of business jargon outside the special activity for which it was intended, in fact, often sounds ridiculous.

In most domestic correspondence and in all international correspondence, jargon should be strictly avoided. Although some terms, such as *hedge* and *red ink*, have become so familiar that they usually don't cause problems in domestic correspondence, they nevertheless reveal the writer's inattention to clear expression and standard English terminology. A professional would try to use precise, correct English at all times.

(Chapter 2 discusses the importance of professionalism in correspondence.)

You have probably received—or have written—letters like the following example. Notice the italicized jargon sprinkled throughout.

> Dear Paul:
>
> Thank you for your letter of concern, Paul. Yes, I do agree that we need to *optimize* sales, but I think we should proceed within the marketing *parameters* already established. If you have other ideas, however, I'd be happy to *bounce them around*.
>
> Perhaps we should have lunch next week. In the meantime, I'll *finalize* the budget, so we'll know what the *bottom line* is. I'll call you on Friday, the fifth, to set up a time to meet.
>
> Best regards,

Even if Paul knows precisely what the writer means, the letter sounds as though the writer is unprofessional and lacks good language skills.

Many people mistakenly believe that using jargon makes them sound very modern and well versed in difficult subjects. This misconception often leads to the excessive use of specialized terminology in nonspecialized letters. The jargon-laden letter just illustrated, for example, could easily have been written in clear, basic language.

> Dear Paul:
>
> Thank you for your letter of concern, Paul. Yes, I do agree that we need to increase sales, but I think we should proceed within the marketing guidelines already established. If you have other ideas, however, I'd be happy to discuss them.

Perhaps we should meet for lunch next week.
In the meantime, I'll finish the budget, so we'll
know what our financial situation is. I'll call you
on Friday, the fifth, to set up a time to meet.

Best regards,

Shop Talk. When jargon is so specialized that it is seldom used outside a particular trade or profession, it is known as *shop talk*. In real estate, for example, *block busting* means obtaining houses below market value by telling residents that someone of a different religion or race is moving in and property values will decline. If you use the term with people outside the real estate profession, however, they may have no idea what you mean. In computer terminology, *wildcard* refers to a group of computerized files. But if you call a group of conventional files *wildcards* in your letter, the reader is not likely to understand.

Buzzwords. Another common type of jargon is the *buzzword*. Terms such as *grow the economy* (to expand it), *granola* (biosphere), and *trash stash* (landfill) are usually imprecise words connected with a specialized field or group. These words are used primarily by people who think they sound important and impressive to laypersons. But their letters would be much clearer and less subject to misinterpretation if they used traditional English. In international correspondence, it is especially imperative to avoid buzzwords.

Gobbledygook. The most imprecise, abstract form of jargon is *gobbledygook*. The name is meant to illustrate the absurdity of jargon at its worst.

Like most other forms of jargon, gobbledygook is used in correspondence when writers mistakenly believe that it makes them sound intelligent and superior to the reader. But it really makes them sound very unprofessional and handicapped by muddled thoughts and weak language skills. Notice the exaggerated complexity and obscure comments in this letter.

Dear Mr. Springer:

In reply to your question regarding the occurrence of casualty and theft losses as applicable to the administration of the estate in reference to the operative Internal Revenue Code that is deemed to be in effect relating to said administration, the bottom line is as follows:

Losses incurred for casualty and theft during the administration of the estate are deemed deductible only if said losses have not been claimed on the federal estate tax return (Form 706). Files concerned must finalize a statement to accompany said estate's income tax return waiving the deduction for estate tax purposes.

A sample statement is submitted herewith for perusal.

Thank you for your interest.

Yours truly,

Although this fuzzy, boring letter discusses a complex Internal Revenue Service regulation, it could be restated in a far less confusing and formidable way.

Dear Mr. Springer:

You asked for an explanation of the Internal Revenue Service (IRS) rule on reporting casualty and theft losses that take place while you are administering an estate. This is what the IRS rule means:

Assume that a casualty or theft loss occurs while you are administering an estate. If this loss is deducted on the estate's federal tax return (Form 706), it can't be deducted somewhere else. To avoid this problem, you could include a statement with the estate's income tax return waiving the deduction for estate tax purposes.

A sample statement that you can use as a guide is enclosed.

I hope this answers your question. If you need more information, please let me know, and I'll be happy to discuss it with you further.

Sincerely,

Examples of Jargon. The following terms are examples of jargon. If you find them used in your letters in a nontechnical context, substitute ordinary, traditional English.

Jargon	Ordinary English
abort	discontinue
access	enter; retrieve
cap	limit
crossover	success in more than one area
downsize	reduce
eta	estimated time of arrival
your eyes only	confidential
fallout	consequences
fast track	quick way to . . .
frame of reference	viewpoint; theory
freeze	hold at the present position
input	ideas or information that is provided
interface	connection; meeting
operative	determining; important
rollover	reinvestment
smart money	those who know best
user friendly	easy to learn and use
window	opportunity

Sections 45 and 46 have examples of slang and cliches, some of which could also be considered a form of jargon.

43. LEARN TO RECOGNIZE OUTDATED, TRITE EXPRESSIONS

A lot of the expressions that you see in letters are trite and shouldn't be used. Cliches, such as "barking up the wrong tree" and "fresh as a daisy," are familiar examples of dull, overworked sayings. (Refer to Section 46 for more about cliches.) Another type of trite expression is rooted in styles once considered appropriate in formal correspondence.

From Formality to Informality

Writing Style. Long ago, certain phrases, such as "beg to advise," were the mark of a well-mannered person. Now, in domestic correspondence, informality is the rule. Even in international correspondence, where more formality is necessary to avoid offending readers who disapprove of too much familiarity, dull, stiff, outdated expressions are out of place. The necessary formality is achieved through style rather than trite expressions.

Notice the many awkward, overly formal expressions in this letter.

My dear Mr. Kingston:

Replying to your letter of the fourth, I want to advise that we shall be pleased to have you visit our offices next Tuesday at ten in the forenoon.

Enclosed please find a map of recent date to direct you in the event you are unfamiliar with our locale.

Thank you in advance for your interest.

Yours very truly,

This is how the letter would read if all of the stilted expressions were changed.

Dear Mr. Kingston:

Yes, we would be happy to schedule an appointment for you on Tuesday, March 11, at 10 a.m.

A map showing our location at 14 Miller Drive is enclosed. Let us know if you need any additional information.

We'll look forward to seeing you next Tuesday, Mr. Kingston. Thanks for your interest.

Cordially,

Trite Expressions to Avoid

Here are examples of trite expressions that should be avoided in contemporary correspondence, both domestic and foreign. If you're still using any of these examples, either delete them or rephrase your sentences in a clear, informal style, using modern English.

Trite Expression	Modern English
acknowledge receipt of	we received
along these lines	such as . . .
as per, per	as we agreed; according to
at an early date	within one week; by December 4, 1994; etc.
at the present writing	now; at present
don't hesitate to	please
enclosed please find	here is; I am enclosing
encounter difficulty	having trouble
for your consideration	(omit)
in receipt of	we received; thank you for
in the amount	for
in the event that	if; in case
our Miss Hyatt	Ms. Hyatt; our representative, Ms. Hyatt
please be advised that	(omit)

regret to inform you	are sorry that
thank(ing) you in advance	thank you; thanks for your help; thank you very much
under separate cover	by Overnight Express Service; etc.

Such dull, stiff, and often wordy expressions in a letter suggest that the writer is a dull, stiff, often verbose person. In the next example, the italicized trite expressions seem more wordy and unimaginative than formal or old, so they might escape the notice of a careless writer.

Dear Shari,

What a wonderful weekend we had at your summer home! It was *interesting to note* that the nights were so delightfully cool. Both Bill and I loved it.

I'm *forwarding* the ginger tea I promised *under separate cover. In the event that* you like it as much as we do, an order blank is enclosed *herewith.*

Last, but not least, do you have Jennie's phone number? I'm embarrassed to ask, but as you probably discovered, I forgot to take it along.

Thank you so much, Shari, for the best weekend we've had all summer. Hope to see you both soon at our place.

Much love,

Notice how much more professional both the letter and the letter writer sound in this rewrite.

Dear Shari,

What a wonderful weekend we had at your summer home! The nights were so delightfully cool. Both Bill and I loved it.

I'm sending you the ginger tea I promised by priority mail. In case you like it as much as we do, an order blank is enclosed.

I'm embarrassed to ask, but do you have Jennie's phone number? As you probably discovered, I forgot to take it along.

Thank you so much, Shari, for the best weekend we've had all summer. Hope to see you both soon at our place.

Much love,

Review the list in Section 46 for more examples of tired language.

44. Shun Pompous Words and Expressions

No one likes a show-off. People who try to impress others by using pretentious language in their correspondence are only fooling themselves. Readers are more likely to think that they sound like pompous bores.

Simple versus Complex English

Some letter writers believe that only simpletons use simple words. Nothing could be further from the truth, as Section 32 demonstrates. By today's standards, the ability to use clear, simple English to describe difficult subjects is an indication that a letter writer has superb language skills, something that is characteristic of an intelligent, educated professional. Simple language, therefore, should not be equated with simple concepts or simplistic thinking.

Guidelines. To avoid appearing pompous in your letters, follow these guidelines.

- Don't use technical or specialized terms (*feedback*) in general correspondence when nonspecialized terms (*comments*) are available. See Section 42.
- Don't use Latin or foreign expressions (*bona fide*) when English terms (*genuine*) are available.
- Don't use unnecessarily complex multisyllable words (*multitudinous*) when simpler one- or two-syllable words (*many*) are available. See Section 32.

Unjustified Use of Pretentious Language. Although skilled letter writers know when to add variety to their correspondence, the writer in the following letter seems to be showing off. The pretentious language can't be justified as necessary for variety.

Dear Mrs. Tremont:

Thank you for your inquiry concerning fulfillment of your August 3 order.

In approximately four weeks we shall commence shipment of fall orders through customary channels. We are cognizant, however, that you must consummate your designs in one month, and thus we are endeavoring to facilitate your shipment with advance scheduling. I shall inform you of the rescheduled shipping date when known.

Please advise if we can be of further assistance.

Sincerely yours,

The letter is so overloaded with pompous words and expressions that it loses all credibility. To rephrase in simple, basic English:

Dear Mrs. Tremont:

Thank you for asking about the shipping date for your August 3 order.

We expect to begin shipping by UPS ground transportation in about four weeks. However, we know that you must finish your designs in one month, so we will try to send your supplies sooner. I'll let you know the exact shipping date on Friday, August 27.

Thank you for your patience, Mrs. Tremont. We appreciate your business and will do our best to meet your deadline.

Cordially,

Examples of Pompous Language. The next list has examples of pompous words and expressions that you should avoid in your letters. Unless you have a legitimate reason to use the longer, more complex term, such as to add more variety and avoid monotonous repetition of the shorter version, use the preferred expression that follows each example.

Pompous Expression	Preferred Expression
aggregation	total
apropos of	with regard to; concerning
carte blanche	unconditional power or authority
cognizant	aware
customary channels	usual way
en rapport	in agreement
facilitate	ease; help
feedback	comments
functionalization	use
input	advice; information
inter alia	among other things
interface with	meet with
milieu	environment; surroundings

obfuscate	confuse
obviate	do away with; prevent
persona grata	fully acceptable
raison d'être	reason for
remuneration	pay
sine qua non	essential
utilize, utilization	use

Other forms of pretentious language include jargon, when used outside the workplace (Section 42), and the stiff, trite expressions previously associated with formal correspondence (Section 43).

45. STAY AWAY FROM SLANG EXPRESSIONS

No one likes to see slang in letters except the people who use it. Those who don't use it wonder if the writer isn't educated or intelligent enough to use proper English or is just typically a crude person. Neither reputation is helpful personally or professionally, so that reason alone should make most people want to avoid slang expressions. In international correspondence, it is essential to avoid slang, because this type of language is unfamiliar to people in other countries and often can't be found in the dictionaries they use for translation.

American Slang

Depending on the source, American slang is variously defined as crude, outrageous, facetious, extravagant, informal, or nonstandard English. It's often all of those things. Slang is a vocabulary coined by special groups, such as computer technicians, schoolchildren, or street gangs. Slang is loved by some groups for its newness or its shock value. It's something that gives them recognition and an identity apart from mainstream society.

Although slang depends on newness for its appeal, sometimes it survives long enough to become business jargon (*dorfed up*), an overworked cliche (*bring home the bacon*) or idiomatic English (*comeback*). Most of the time it disappears and is replaced by something newer and, often, more outrageous.

Recognizing Slang

The really outrageous or obscene expressions are easy to recognize, and few people would use such language in business or social correspondence. But if you think of slang as any nonstandard language, such as jargon and cliches, you may be less aware of it. All sorts of nonstandard language are common in American society. (Refer to the other sections in this chapter for a general cross-section.) Careless writers often let such language slip into their correspondence, as shown by the italicized phrases in the following letter.

Dear Fred:

Here are the latest statistics on employee absenteeism. My boss has had them *in cold storage* until he could verify the sudden increase last quarter.

I believe we need to take immediate steps to *turn this around*. Although further study will be needed, one thing we can do right away is exercise more control in our hiring procedures. I realize that your department has not been taking everyone who *comes down the pike*, but we may need more emphasis on reference checking and psychological previews.

Let me know if you have any suggestions, Fred. Thanks very much.

Best regards,

The three italicized slang expressions are so familiar that they may not seem like slang. But they are. All are among those slang expressions that have survived over several decades. Replacing them with standard English:

Dear Fred:

Here are the latest statistics on employee absenteeism. My boss had been holding them until he could verify the sudden increase last quarter.

I believe we need to take immediate steps to reverse this trend. Although further study will be needed, one thing we can do right away is exercise more control in our hiring procedures. I realize that your department has not hired everyone who ever applied, but we may need more emphasis on reference checking and psychological previews.

Let me know if you have any suggestions, Fred. Thanks very much.

Best regards,

The slang used in personal letters is often more crude than that used in business or social letters. Notice some of the italicized phrases.

Dear Tom:

How's college life treating you? I hope being a *BMOC* isn't wearing you down!

Nothing much happening here. But do you remember that *hot little babe* we met over Labor Day weekend? Well, I got up enough *guts* to ask her out, and we're going out again next weekend. She was dating a real *airhead*, so I think she considers me a *genius!*

> Write when you can, Tom, and let me know
> how you like Penn State.

Yours,

When friends use slang in everyday conversation, is it appropriate for them also to use it in letters to each other? Language experts would frown on slang in either speech or writing. But it's understandable that someone who always uses casual language in speech wouldn't want to become a totally different person in writing. Fortunately, it's possible to remain casual and conversational without replying on slang expressions.:

Dear Tom:

> How's college life treating you? I hope being the most popular man on campus isn't wearing you down!
>
> Nothing much is happening here. But do you remember that gorgeous blonde we met over Labor Day weekend? Well, I got up enough nerve to ask her out, and we're going out again next weekend. She was dating someone who wasn't too bright, so I think she considers me a genius!
>
> Write when you can, Tom, and let me know how you like Penn State.

Yours,

Slang Expressions to Avoid

Anyone who wants to sound like a literate, intelligent professional will always choose standard English over nonstandard English. Slang has no place in social or business correspondence. As you can see from the previous example, it also can be eliminated from personal correspondence without giving friends the impression that you have a split personality. With a little practice, you can write letters that are friendly, casual, and conversational without peppering every paragraph with slang.

Examine your correspondence for both new and old slang expressions such as the following and substitute standard English as illustrated in the previous examples.

Slang	Standard English
belly up	die or collapse
chicken out	lose nerve
dead in the water	stalled
eyeball to eyeball	face to face
full of bull	wrong
get a kick out of	enjoy
hands down	easily
hit the road	leave
jump down someone's throat	respond aggressively
make a big deal out of	overreact
nail to the wall	make an example of
out to lunch	crazy or eccentric
pissed off	angry
play hardball	be extremely intent and serious
put the screws to	use extreme pressure on
raise hell	celebrate boisterously
run out of steam	stall
take a beating	pay too much
up to speed	meeting established standards
warts and all	everything including imperfections
weenie	ineffectual person

Since many slang expressions that remain in use become overworked cliches, refer to Section 46 for more examples of undesirable, nonstandard language.

46. EXCISE TIRESOME AND UNIMAGINATIVE CLICHES

Cliches—listless, banal expressions—are alive and well in both domestic and international correspondence. Although these often imprecise expressions may seem harmless, they are puzzling to foreign readers who can't translate expressions such as *out on a limb* literally.

Even domestic readers get tired of hearing the same old expressions over and over. Cliches make a writer appear unimaginative and unprofessional. For more about a different type of tired, old-fashioned language, refer to the list of trite expressions in Section 43.

Are Cliches All Bad?

Does the tiresome nature of cliches mean that they should be strictly forbidden in all correspondence, even in personal letters? It might be impossible to relegate them to oblivion, although English purists would like to do exactly that.

In informal correspondence, a cliche can occasionally be used for special effect or as a pun or in irony. If the U.S. dollar, for example, happened to be weak and unstable at some time, you might say that a questionable line of reasoning is as "sound as the dollar," meaning that it is really a weak argument. But in business and social correspondence, clear, straightforward English is always preferred.

The fact that cliches are overworked expressions means that they have been around a long time. Some began as slang or business jargon. Others were created as proverbs. In all cases, the more they were used, the more banal, dull, and unimaginative they seemed. Only occasionally would a cliche gain respectability as a basic, standard term. *A-1*, for instance, is a standard rating label in some organizations, and *arm's length* is a standard term in labor relations. But even in those cases, the expressions resume their status as a cliche when they are used repeatedly in other situations.

Cliches in Correspondence

Cliches are more prevalent in correspondence than slang, business jargon, and other undesirable language. (Some expressions would fit into all or most of the categories.) Although many people avoid the obvious cliches, such as *back to the drawing board*, they regularly—and usually unknowingly—use others, such as *vicious circle*.

Notice that some of the italicized cliches in this letter are just overworked expressions rather than the proverbial kind of remark, such as *a bird in the hand is worth two in the bush*.

> Dear Fran,
>
> How I wish we could join you for dinner on Tuesday, the tenth. But Ed and I promised Cindy that we would attend her first recital that evening. Ed, of course, *couldn't care less* about a recital, but Cindy is the *apple of his eye*, so he agreed to go.
>
> I'm so glad you asked, though, because it reminded me that we haven't seen you and Dick in a long time. We really appreciate your thinking of us, and *sooner or later*, I know we'll all find a free night.
>
> Take care.
>
> Love from us,

Letters with cliches can easily be rewritten without losing their conversational quality. The belief that cliches are necessary to sound friendly and casual is a fiction, as this rewrite illustrates.

Dear Fran,

How I wish we could join you for dinner on Tuesday, the tenth. But Ed and I promised Cindy that we would attend her first recital that evening. Ed, of course, doesn't care about recitals, but you know how proud he is of anything Cindy does, so he agreed to go.

I'm so glad you asked, though, because it reminded me that we haven't seen you and Dick in a long time. We really appreciate your thinking of us, and eventually, I know we'll all find a free night.

Take care.

Love from us,

Since businesspeople need to be businesslike and professional in their correspondence, the use of cliches can be a serious mistake. Tired, overworked expressions weaken a message, and weak messages are ineffective messages. The following letter, for example, doesn't sound professional. It's an apology for a late reply to someone's letter, but because it doesn't sound serious and businesslike, the reader may wonder whether the delay occurred because the writer just isn't a very responsible person.

Dear Mr. Harcourt:

Please forgive my delay in replying to your letter asking about the zoning study. I've been out *beating the bushes* for new business, and my secretary has been on maternity leave. So the mail has been reaching me *hit or miss*.

I expect to *dot the final i's and cross the final t's* on the study next week. While on the road this past week, I *strayed from the beaten path* long enough to collect some information from our Houston office. As a result, I now have enough facts to *make a stab* at the analysis.

I'll call you next Monday to let you know when I can *wrap up* the analysis. In the meantime, please accept my apologies if this late reply to your letter has caused you any concern.

Cordially,

This rewrite eliminates the cliches and substitutes straight-forward, businesslike language.

Dear Mr. Harcourt:

Please forgive my delay in replying to your letter asking about the zoning study. I've been away on business, and my secretary has been on maternity leave. So the mail has been late reaching me.

I expect to complete the study by July 1. While traveling this past week, I stopped at our Houston office and collected some essential information. As a result, I now have enough facts to do a reliable analysis.

I'll call you next Monday to let you know when I will finish the analysis. In the meantime, please accept my apologies if this late reply to your letter has caused you any concern.

Cordially,

Familiar Cliches

The following list has examples of cliches used so often that you may be including them in your letters out of habit. Study your correspondence and eliminate the expressions that detract from the clarity and freshness of your comments.

Familiar Expression	Meaning
all in the same boat	all sharing a similar experience
at one's fingertips	readily available
axe to grind	seeking a particular objective
back to the drawing board	redesign or start over
beat around the bush	approach indirectly
beside the point	irrelevant
bottom line	result
business as usual	continuing in the face of difficulty
clear the air	remove complications and misunderstandings
conventional wisdom	generally accepted view
fair shake	fair treatment
food for thought	something to consider
get to the bottom of	find the underlying reasons for
in a nutshell	briefly
know the ropes	know how to do something
long shot	little chance of success
muddy the water	confuse things
point of no return	too late to change
rule of thumb	general guide
shot in dark	conjecture
sound as a dollar	reliable
tip of the iceberg	only the beginning
whole new ball game	new or different situation

Refer to Sections 42 and 43 for more examples of overused expressions.

47. AVOID WORDS THAT OFFEND

People who generally have good manners wouldn't intentionally write a letter that offends someone. Usually, they would try to make the reader feel good by saying nice things and choosing words that have a pleasing, positive effect. Refer to Section 27 in Chapter 4 for tips on being tactful and diplomatic in your letters.

Some words, such as *appreciate*, just naturally have a positive effect. They increase our self-esteem, give us confidence, promote a sense of well-being, or simply make us momentarily happy and content. But many other words, when used in a certain context, have the opposite effect. Those are the words that offend.

Negative Words and Expressions

Some words are fighting words; they make people angry or rebellious. Other words may not have a critical or offensive connotation, but they suggest pessimism, which in turn suggests that a letter writer lacks confidence. Both types of words are negative and counterproductive in correspondence because they encourage a negative response. This letter, for example, is spoiled by poor word choice that creates a negative tone.

Dear Mrs. Torreyana:

I received your letter saying that the program was ready and that an advance copy was enclosed. But I'm afraid you forgot to enclose it.

Please rush me a copy immediately by overnight express. Without it, I'll be forced to postpone my report to the Board of Directors.

Thank you.

Sincerely,

Although the letter doesn't call Mrs. Torreyana stupid or irresponsible, it won't make her feel happy. It probably will make her think that the writer is a cold, unpleasant person who is hard to work with.

Negative words seldom motivate people to perform better; they are more likely to create resentment and dissatisfaction and cause people to become defensive. This rewrite makes the essential point—that the program was not enclosed and the writer urgently needs it—without creating ill feelings.

> Dear Mrs. Torreyana:
>
> Thank you for letting me know that the program is ready. I'm delighted that we'll soon see the results of our many late-night meetings.
>
> The copy of the program you mentioned was not enclosed with your letter, so I'd very much appreciate it if you would rush me a copy by overnight express. I'm scheduled to present the program to the Board of Directors, and the Wednesday meeting is the last one before the conference.
>
> Many thanks for your help, Mrs. Torreyana.
>
> Cordially,

Psychology of Negativity. The psychology behind this emphasis on avoiding negative words is the same as the simple psychology applied in everyday life: You create a better impression and motivate people to do more for you when you're kind and thoughtful toward them. This guideline applies to both personal and professional correspondence. Notice the difference in tone created in the next two letters.

> Dear Perry,
>
> Got your letter about the cabin. Since I don't own it, it's probably a bad idea for you and Frank to go over there alone. My lease doesn't

allow me to give out the keys to anyone. If there were an accident and anything was destroyed, the manager might evict me, and you might get in trouble too.

So we don't have to worry, why don't you wait and we'll all go the first weekend next month? Let me know if both you and Frank can make it then. We'll have a great time.

So long,

All of those negative words—*bad, accident, destroyed, evict, trouble,* and *worry*—give the letter a very unfriendly tone. Even if the writer and reader are accustomed to speaking very bluntly to each other, it never makes sense to be unnecessarily negative. To rephrase:

Dear Perry,

Thanks for your letter asking about you and Frank using the cabin. Is there any chance that you and Frank could join me at the cabin the first weekend next month?

I know you mentioned an earlier weekend, but a clause in my lease says that I have to be there when the cabin is in use. Anyway, we've all been talking about getting together this summer--so why not do it?

Ask Frank, and let me know what you think. It would be great to see you both again, so I'm hoping your answer will be yes.

See you soon,

In spite of the examples just given, a potentially negative word may be the appropriate choice in some cases. If you're writing to your insurance company about an accident, for instance, you will presumably have to use the word *accident* at least once or perhaps several times. If you're writing about a death in the family, you obviously won't use cheery, upbeat language but will select quiet, dignified words appropriate for the occasion. Common sense must always be your guide in word choice.

Examples of Negative Words. Most of the time you have a choice whether to be negative or positive in your letters. In those cases, phrase your comments to avoid negative words such as the following.

abhor	menial
absurd	misrepresent
afraid	naive
allege	radical
careless	ruin
claim	senseless
demand	squander
deplore	stubborn
destroy	timid
fail	troublesome
false	unfair
fault	useless
incompetent	waste
insist	weak
mediocre	wrong

Discriminatory Words and Expressions

Some words and expressions offend because they imply that the other person is inferior. The words alone may not be offensive, but in a particular context they may suggest that a letter writer has feelings of bias or disrespect.

Whether a person is telling an ethnic joke that demeans a particular group or is using discriminatory language in conversation and correspondence, the result is the same. Any expression that is insensitive to someone else's feelings should be strictly avoided.

Follow any changes in equal employment opportunity laws and other programs and laws that affect an organization's practices concerning racial, disability, and sexual discrimination.

Racial and Ethnic Bias. Opinions differ in regard to the acceptable description for different racial and ethnic groups. Some people prefer the term *black*, for example, whereas others use the term *African-American*. Nevertheless, some guidelines can safely be followed in your letters.

- Don't refer to someone's color (the *black* minister) unless it serves a necessary or significant purpose (the *first black* minister ever to serve in Winterhaven).
- Beware of adjectives such as *quiet* or *intelligent* in association with racial or ethnic identification. ("Mrs. Chavez is an *intelligent Mexican-American* secretary in our Los Angeles office.") To some, this will wrongly imply that the opposite is usually true, that Mexican-Americans are not usually intelligent.
- Avoid segregating everyone into white and nonwhite groups. ("Our company has a program for *nonwhites*.") Specify the actual heritages involved. ("Our company has a program for *African-American, Asian-American*, and other heritages.")
- Don't use words that might humiliate someone. ("This rebate is for poor minorities.") Specify the particular heritages involved. ("This rebate is for *Mexican-American* and *African-American* employees.")

Disability Bias. Terminology changes from time to time, and different organizations prefer different terms to describe disabled individuals. In the 1990s, both *disabled* and *physically challenged* are common terms. (Avoid use of the term *handicapped*.) Regardless of current terminology, don't focus your attention on a person's disability in your letters; the disabled person would probably rather be treated the same as anyone else. Here are a few do's and don'ts.

- Focus on a person's abilities (good organizational skills), but don't mention the disabilities (speech and hearing impairment), unless it is essential to the discussion. Then refer to it only as an incidental point. ("Joe Dexter, who is himself a paraplegic, will discuss office designs for disabled employees.")
- Don't use words such as *fit* (seizure), *crippled* (disabled), or *retarded* (mentally disabled). (Note, however, that preferred terminology changes from time to time.)
- Don't go to the opposite extreme and treat a major disability as nothing or as a joke (your *little problem*).

Sexual Bias. The same insensitivity that leads to discrimination against racial and ethnic groups and the disabled also causes sexism. Many people do not realize that they are using discriminatory language in their letters. The following guidelines apply to the most common types of sexual bias, such as the implication that women are inferior to men or that they are recognized for their physical characteristics rather than their personal or professional abilities.

- If you address men by a personal or professional title, also address women that way (*Mr.* Hill and *Ms.* Kerrey; Cliff and Anne).
- Avoid references to "husbands" and "wives" (the candidates and their *spouses*).
- Use asexual words for general references (*humankind; society; civilization; people*).
- Refer to a woman according to her abilities (*capable*), not her physical characteristics (*pretty*) in a professional context (my *capable* assistant, Ms. Edwards).
- Don't mention that a particular employee is a woman (the *woman* programmer) unless it is essential or significant (the *first woman* ever to win the Bentley scholarship).

The other sections in this chapter have more examples of language that should be avoided in your correspondence.

48. KNOW WHEN COLLOQUIAL LANGUAGE IS APPROPRIATE

Colloquial English is the very informal English that is used in everyday conversation among family members and close friends: "Hey, how're you doin'?" It includes all the familiar words and expressions, such as "take it easy" and "see you," that are readily exchanged in person but are used only in very informal letters. Slang and cliches are included in the informal expressions characteristic of colloquial English.

Colloquial English in Letters

Colloquial English is used in letters, but whether it *should* be is a matter of disagreement among language authorities. English instructors generally believe that colloquial English should be confined to correspondence between family members and very close friends.

Domestic business and social correspondence is casual and conversational—to a point. As the previous sections in this chapter emphasized, however, it should not be so casual that it includes slang, cliches, and other informal language. Even letters to family members and close friends need not include such language to be friendly and casual.

The difference between colloquial language and other forms of language may not seem clear at all times. Some things, such as contractions, are found in both colloquial and more formal writing. The principal difference is that colloquial English allows just about anything, but standard business and social correspondence eliminates very casual, nonstandard language.

This letter is written in colloquial English.

Dear Ben,

    How's it goin? I just thought I'd write to say I got the video you loaned me and think it's really cool. Man, you must have splurged. Those things aren't cheap.

I don't mean to bug you, but if you're through with the one I sent last month, I wouldn't mind having it back.

Well, so long for now. Take it easy over spring break!

Later,

The next letter is a revised version that retains the casual, friendly tone but omits the obvious colloquialisms.

Dear Ben,

I got the video you sent and wanted to let you know that I loved it. I'm sure it was expensive, so thanks for loaning it to me.

Have you had a chance to look at the tape I sent last month? How did you like it? When you're done, would you mind returning it? I'd like to see it again myself.

Have a great time during spring break! Hope to hear from you soon.

All the best,

Examples of Colloquial English. The following expressions are a few examples of colloquial English.

brainy	hunch
every which way	in back of
flunk	kid
funny (odd)	make no bones about
get away with	slob
go for	snooze
gumption	stump (puzzle)
guy	

Provincialisms

Difference between Provincialisms and Colloquialisms. A word or expression that is peculiar to a particular geographic region or area is a *provincialism*. This type of dialectal or local word, expression, or idiom is a type of colloquialism (in general, a colloquialism is not confined to particular regions or parts of the country).

Although television and newspapers are helping people in remote parts of the country to know more about the language of people in other areas, some expressions are not known in every region. You may have heard someone say "chuck it," meaning throw it away, or "walk a piece," meaning walk a distance. Or you may have heard someone use *anywheres* for *anywhere*, *calculate* for *think*, or *tote* for *carry*. Often the people who use such provincialisms in their letters are unaware that the expressions aren't used or known everywhere else.

When Provincialisms May Be Used. Provincialisms, like colloquialisms, should not be used outside of very informal correspondence between family members and close friends. A serious problem with using them even in such correspondence, however, is that they may become a habit. If they do become a habit, they will also find their way into other personal, business, or social correspondence.

Because provincialisms are words and expressions that may be familiar only to the others who live in a particular part of the country and because they are substitutes for standard English, they should be strictly avoided in most correspondence. Foreign readers, especially, might not easily translate a provincialism. For more about writing international correspondence, refer to Chapter 6.

6

Writing International Messages

---

49. USE LITERAL LANGUAGE

Most writers compose international messages in the same way that they compose domestic messages. They shouldn't, however, because writing to someone in Okayama, Japan; Tegucigalpa, Honduras; or Oujda, Morocco, is not the same as writing to someone in New York, Chicago, or Los Angeles. The readers in other countries have very different cultural, social, religious, political, and business practices, and they don't always understand—or approve of—modern American practices. Moreover, they may not even speak English or have adequate translation services.

In spite of the many differences between domestic and international correspondence, however, one thing remains the same: Letter writers format international messages in the same way that they format domestic messages. Formatting instructions are given in Section 5 in Chapter 1 and Sections 55 and 56 in Chapter 7. Section 58 in Chapter 7 describes the principal parts of letters, such as the inside address, and points out any differences between the style for domestic and international correspondence.

The Need to Be Precise

Your letters must be very clear and precise—a good policy in any situation—if the reader is from another culture and either doesn't know English or knows it only as a second or third language. If you've ever studied another language or tried to translate a letter written in another language, you'll know that the translation process is almost a word-by-word exercise.

In translating a foreign language, you probably looked up many of the words in a foreign-language dictionary and, for each word, wrote down the literal meaning or equivalent English term. Since you were likely struggling just to define each word and form sentences, any attempt at humor by the writer no doubt escaped your attention or simply sounded strange. Making sense out of the text was about all you could handle without having to worry about reading between the lines or picking up the writer's nuances.

Foreign readers will respond in the same way to your correspondence. It will be enough of a struggle for them to translate simple, straightforward English without having to cope with American idioms, satire, and other forms of language unfamiliar to them. Whatever you say, therefore, they will interpret literally, just as you would do if the situation were reversed.

Problem Language

We need to remind ourselves every time we write a letter that foreign readers have a lot of trouble handling any type of language that is difficult to translate literally or is hard to find in a dictionary. Oxymorons, acronyms, double entendres, grammatical errors—all of these things must be edited out of international correspondence. Nontraditional English, such as trendy expressions and neologisms, the subject of Section 50, and jargon, slang, and cliches, discussed in Chapter 5, are equally troublesome to a non-English-language reader.

Humor. If your letters contain statements meant to be witty, facetious, satirical, or playful, don't count on the reader being able to understand or appreciate your humorous bent. A literal translation may produce a completely different meaning. Consider this letter from an American trying to use a light touch in response to a contract cancellation by a foreign customer. The second letter eliminates the objectionable language and other problems.

Dear Mr. Nnaji:

That was quite a bomb you delivered in your last letter! It took me most of the morning to scrape the pieces off the wall. But I have concluded that you did the right thing. In view of our delivery problems, we deserved to get blown apart.

I've talked to the manager of our Shipping Department, however, and he believes he has a solution that will immediately put an end to the problem of late deliveries. I'll call you next week to discuss the matter further. I'm sure we can provide satisfactory service in the future.

Best regards,

Dear Mr. Nnaji:

I was very sorry to receive your letter stating that you want to cancel our contract to supply diesel parts to your company. However, I understand your concern about the late delivery of four recent shipments.

The manager of our Shipping Department believes he has a solution. He thinks that he can now end the problem of late deliveries.

I will telephone you on March 16 to tell you what we can do to solve this problem. I know we can now fill your orders promptly.

> Our company values your business, and I hope
> we can continue to supply the diesel parts you
> need.
>
> Very sincerely yours,

If the first letter were sent, the writer shouldn't be surprised if the recipient believes that he or she has just been accused of a crime—delivery of a letter *bomb* that explodes while the mail is being opened. To an American, however, the word bomb means not only an explosive device but also a shock or a failure. The exclamation mark, in fact, is a typical American device used to signal that a comment isn't meant to be taken literally or seriously. The phrase "scrape the pieces off the wall" is an informal term sometimes used in a certain context to mean collecting one's thoughts again or recovering from a shock. "Blown apart" is another American slang term for being defeated. But none of these interpretations is likely to be known by a foreign reader who probably has only a standard English dictionary for reference.

Although a reader may have a moderately good grasp of modern U.S. English, humor is still risky. The reader may come from a culture that frowns on the use of humor with strangers or in initial contacts. Using humor may make it seem as though you are trying to be too familiar, which will be interpreted as a sign of disrespect.

Even if you write to someone who understands U.S. English and the American tendency to be casual and use a light touch in correspondence, what are the odds that you and the reader will both appreciate the same type of humor? Not very good. Generally, whenever you're tempted to be clever or to inject a light, humorous touch to your international correspondence, *don't.*

Oxymorons. Some letter writers like to add life and color to their correspondence by using *oxymorons*, or contradictory terms, such as *honest thief* or *sweet sorrow*. At times, a contradictory description may seem appropriate. You may have bittersweet thoughts—a combination of unpleasant and pleasant thoughts—about a place you visited or a project you worked on.

Most English-speaking people who have good language skills understand and may even enjoy reading an occasional oxymoron in the letters they receive. Foreign readers, however, are usually perplexed by them. They would prefer that you be clear and straightforward rather than clever and colorful. A lot of the embellishments and poetic flourishes that writers skillfully weave into their letters are lost anyway during translation into another language.

Consider the next example. The oxymoron *moderately grand* in the first letter may sound interesting, but the simple English in the second letter is more precise and clear and will make much more sense to a foreign reader. The second version also improves the general composition.

Dear Mrs. de Lima:

Thank you for your modestly grand proposal to exchange your junior personnel with ours in several departments for one month. I'll give it my utmost attention and will send you my decision as soon as possible.

Cordially,

Dear Mrs. de Lima:

Thank you for your detailed proposal. The plan to exchange your junior personnel with ours in three departments for one month is interesting.

I will study your idea carefully and send you my thoughts by February 11. I know that we will both benefit from your efforts.

Sincerely,

The following are examples of oxymorons.

agreeably disagreeable	mildly aggressive
apparent uncertainty	narrow expanse
blind vision	openly confining
calmly aroused	restless relaxation
conflicting agreement	selfish indulgence
curious indifference	slow acceleration
frankly insidious	unfair justice

To avoid confusion or misinterpretation by a non-English reader, examine your correspondence for unintentional oxymorons or those you insert out of habit. Substitute a noncontradictory phrase or recast the entire sentence if necessary.

Abbreviations. In general, abbreviations should never be used in international correspondence. The term *abbreviations* includes acronyms pronounced like a word (BASIC) and initialisms pronounced by initial letters (*asap*). Many foreign readers won't know what the abbreviations mean and may not be able to find them in a standard dictionary. Also, don't expect your readers to have a dictionary of English abbreviations; many English-speaking Americans don't even have one.

The one exception to the rule never to use abbreviations in international correspondence is in the case of excessive repetition of certain names. If your letter repeats the name of an organization, a product, or a program over and over, it is permissible to spell out the name the first time used and put the abbreviation for it in parentheses immediately after the name. Thereafter, the abbreviation alone may be used. For example:

Dear Mr. Sainju:

Thank you for asking about the Watson Gutter Guard (WGG). Here is the sample you requested. The design and quality of this small piece is the same as the design and quality of the actual guard.

The WGG has been sold in forty-seven countries
on four continents. Details about the WGG are
given in the enclosed booklet.

Please write or telephone if you have any
questions. We appreciate your interest.

Sincerely yours,

This practice of using abbreviations for succeeding references to names or titles does not apply to the repetition of
ordinary words such as *administration*.

If you are writing to someone in another country and are
enclosing printed literature, a report, or tables that already
contain abbreviations, such as *ml* (milliliter) or *gal.* (gallon),
attach a list of abbreviations used in the material showing the
spelled-out version of each one.

Idioms. Few things give foreign readers a headache as
quickly as American *idioms*, words and expressions peculiar
to the language. Because they don't conform to the basic rules
of grammar and usually can't be translated easily or literally,
they should be avoided in international correspondence.
Think of someone who doesn't understand English but is trying to translate a letter with phrases such *as back out of, as far
as,* and *stands to reason*.

Dear Mrs. Asante:

Thank you for the copy of our new lease dated
June 21, 1995.

Although we don't want to back out of the
lease, we would like to suggest two changes. As
far as the first clause is concerned, I believe that
the last sentence should be deleted. It stands to
reason that the second clause should therefore be
made part of the first clause.

Please let me know if you will agree to these changes. Thanks for your help.

Sincerely,

Such idioms are not likely to be in a foreign reader's standard dictionary, and they do not fit in the limited understanding the reader may have of the basic parts of speech in the English language. To make your letters understandable to a non-English-speaking reader, rewrite any sentences containing an idiom. Rewriting the previous letter and deleting the idioms improves the composition.

Dear Mrs. Asante:

Thank you for the copy of our June 21, 1995, lease.

We are happy that we may use the building described in the lease. However, we want to suggest two changes in the agreement. We make this request since one sentence does not apply to us. We therefore propose the following:

1. Delete the last sentence in the first clause.

2. Incorporate the second clause into the first clause.

Please telephone or write if you will accept these changes. Thank you for your help.

Sincerely,

The following are examples of English idioms:

aim to prove	on its way out
as regards	on the face of it
back down	out of place
by the way	pressed for time
can't help feeling	a rash of
change one's mind	rough time
free from	see daylight
have in mind	see it through
hold back	sense of proportion
in the same vein	slip one's mind
kind of	take one's time
leave a lot to be desired	take time off
make time for	time is running out
no way	with an eye toward
off-hand	year end, year out

Grammar books and writing guides often have detailed lists of idioms. Also, you may be able to find a complete book of idioms in your local library.

Grammatical Errors. Grammatical errors in a letter will always create translation problems for a foreign reader. Such problems include errors in grammatical usage, punctuation, and spelling. Certain errors, such as misplaced modifiers, are especially common in correspondence. Other common errors include the incorrect use of the parts of speech, such as using an adjective when an adverb is required. Chapter 2 describes the importance of using good grammar, clear punctuation, consistent capitalization, and correct spelling and word division.

A misplaced modifier creates one of the worst translation nightmares for foreign readers. Some writers unknowingly dangle many modifiers in their letters. For example: *"Working on a new schedule,* the idea occurred to me." The clause "Working on a new schedule" appears to modify *idea.* But that doesn't make sense. Ideas don't work on schedules; people do. So the sentence needs to be rewritten: *"Working on a new schedule, I thought of this idea."* Or: "I thought of this idea while working on a new schedule."

You may think that any reader would eventually realize what is meant. But no one should have to deliberate over another person's careless grammar.

Confusable Words. Incorrect word choice is another detraction from literal English. In this case, a letter writer picks not a vague or imprecise word but a totally incorrect word. Someone might write the noun *advice* when the verb *advise* would have been the correct choice.

Here are examples of terms that are often confused and misused. In some cases, the confusion occurs because the words sound similar but are spelled differently and have different meanings (homophones). In other cases, the confusion results from a misunderstanding of the difference in meaning between two terms. For example:

- The noun *ability* refers to a physical or mental power to do something: "His *ability* to solve complex equations is remarkable." The noun *capacity* refers to a physical measure of content: "The truck has a two-ton *capacity*."
- With the homophones *affect* and *effect,* the verb *affect* means to influence: "Will this delay *affect* your program?" The noun *effect* means a result: "What *effect* will this delay have on your program?"
- The preposition *among* refers to a relationship of more than two things: "Opinions were exchanged *among* the three employees." The preposition *between* refers to a relationship of two things or more than two when each one is individually related to all the others: "The debate was *between* the Republicans and the Democrats."
- The noun *balance* refers to the equality of totals: "The account *balance* is $2.18." The noun *remainder* refers to what is left over: "The *remainder* of the newsletters will be mailed today."

- With the homophones *complement* and *compliment*, the verb *complement* means to complete: "The new carpeting *complements* the design." The verb *compliment* means to flatter or praise: "I want to *compliment* you for doing such a good job."
- The verb *imply* means to suggest by inference or association: "We don't want to *imply* that all of the parts were defective." The verb *infer* means to reach a conclusion based on the facts or circumstances: "We might *infer* from the study that the entire population is at risk."
- The noun *libel* refers to printed or written defamation that injures someon's reputation: "The newspaper accusation constitutes *libel*." The noun *slander* refers to oral defamation that injures someone's reputation: "His accusation at the party constitutes *slander*."
- With the homophones *principal* and *principle*, the adjective *principal* means main or important: "The *principal* reason for expanding is greater profits." The noun *principle* refers to a rule, doctrine, or assumption: "The *principle* of weightlessness is described in the new book."
- With the homophones *stationary* and *stationery*, the adjective *stationary* means fixed or immobile: "The platform is *stationary*." The noun *stationery* refers to writing paper, envelopes, and related materials: "The company has attractive *stationery*."
- The adjective *viable* means capable of existing: "The new company is a *viable* enterprise." The adjective *workable* means capable of working or succeeding: "The plan is *workable*."

Refer to Chapter 5 and to Section 50 in this chapter for more examples of serious language problems in international correspondence, such as slang, jargon, cliches, and neologisms.

50. USE TRADITIONAL ENGLISH

The need to use standard, traditional English is obvious from the discussions in Chapter 5 and Section 49 of this chapter. Not only should you avoid the language described there—jargon, idioms, and other expressions that create translation problems for foreign readers—but you should also avoid non-traditional expressions, such as trendy words and euphemisms.

English Around the World

In other countries, English is taught in many schools, and it is the principal language of international trade. But the question is: which English is the *real* international English? The answer depends on the country. English in the United States, for example, is different in some ways from English in the United Kingdom.

Among the differences between U.S. and U.K. English is the treatment of words as singular or plural. Americans treat some words as singular (*government is*), whereas in the United Kingdom they are plural (*government are*). Some terms have different meanings. In the United States "tabling a motion" means putting it aside; in United Kingdom terminology it means acting on something immediately. Vocabulary differs too. In the United States you would *lease* an apartment or office; in the United Kingdom you would *let* it. Spelling differences in the United Kingdom include the transposition of *e* and *r* in words such as center (*centre*) and the addition of *-me* to words such as program (*programme*). Some articles, such as *the* (*in the future*), are dropped in the United Kingdom (*in future*).

Countries in which English is a second or third language may also adopt U.K. English, or they may develop a completely different form of English. The Japanese, for example, don't have singular and plural versions of words in their own language, so they tend not to distinguish between singular and plural English words. Egyptians sometimes treat English adjectives as nouns and then omit the actual noun: "He works in our American [office]."

With so many different versions of English in the world, it is imperative that American letter writers use only the clearest, simplest, most basic and traditional English possible. If you add contemporary American fashion and American language oddities to the mix of international English, sensible translation and comprehension of your letters in other countries will become virtually impossible.

New Words

Although all countries add new terms to their vocabularies, few can match the love affair that Americans have with trendy words and other neologisms. In the following example, the writer of the first letter uses expressions that a foreign reader might not know or be able to find in a standard English dictionary. Traditional terminology has been substituted and the composition improved in the second letter.

Dear Hamami,

I enjoyed your last letter and all the news about your classes at the university.

I'm writing this letter on my new computer. The typeface looks a lot like yours. The computer is working fine now, but last week I thought my hard disk had crashed. It turned out to be only a loose cable.

I'd like to get a laser printer, but I'm a little tapped out right now. Maybe next year.

Good luck with your accounting course and your exams.

Your friend,

Dear Hamami,

I enjoyed your May 3 letter. Thank you for the news about your classes at the university.

I am using my new computer to write this letter. The typeface looks like the typeface on your computer. My computer is working fine now. Last week, however, I thought the hard disk had failed. But it was only a loose cable.

I would like to buy a laser printer but do not have the money now. I may be able to get one next year.

I wish you much success with your accounting course and your examinations.

Your friend,

Trendy Words. When new words are so new that everyone wants to use them to sound ultramodern, they are faddish, or trendy. Whether they will last long enough eventually to make it into a standard dictionary is doubtful.

Some words are temporary slang terms that are part of the vocabulary of members of street gangs and other youth. Within a year, the pressure to be different causes the terms to vanish as a newer vocabulary is created. Newness is the key. A few terms remain in use, however. The slang term *bad*, for example, meaning good, is still used and is in most slang dictionaries. But imagine writing to someone in another country and using *bad* for *good:* "Your employer is a *bad* [good] manager."

Even if trendy expressions, such as *spin doctor, grow the economy,* and *user friendly,* survive over the long term, they are not likely to be in the traditional English dictionaries used by foreign readers. The rule about using nontraditional English when writing to someone in another country is simple: If a word or expression isn't in a standard, traditional English dictionary, and if it isn't consistent with the traditional rules of English grammar, *don't* use it.

Neologisms. Not all new words are trendy or fashionable at the moment. Some, although relatively new, have nevertheless been around for several years or even several decades. But they are still too new to be part of the traditional English vocabulary that has existed since earlier times in the history of the English-speaking world. They are also too new to have become part of the English vocabulary used in other countries.

Avoid neologisms, such as the following examples, in your international correspondence.

access	fast track
A-list *or* short list	killer technology
couch potatoes	smart card
damage control	

Don't worry if using traditional English instead of neologisms involves more words. In international correspondence, clarity and reader comprehension are more important than brevity or impressing the reader with your modern vocabulary.

Euphemisms. Although *euphemisms,* inoffensive substitutes for potentially offensive expressions, have existed throughout the history of the English language, they have become more widespread in recent decades. The argument in favor of euphemisms is that they may avoid offending someone: "This message will be of interest to all *senior citizens* [old people]." The argument against them is that they sometimes sound silly or pretentious and may be more vague than the original term: "He is indisposed [ill]."

In international correspondence, the same problem that occurs with neologisms occurs with euphemisms. They often make literal translation difficult or impossible, and since the newer euphemisms are not part of the traditional English language, they are not available in the standard dictionaries used by foreign readers.

The following are examples of euphemisms that, in most cases, should be changed to the recommended standard, traditional English in your international correspondence.

Euphemism	Traditional English
appropriate	take
benign neglect	neglect
deep six	destroy
departed	dead
disadvantaged	poor
expire	die
free enterprise	private enterprise
furlough (work)	layoff from work
golden years	old age
indigent	poor
quaint	small
relieve from job	fire
stable growth	slow growth
traffic expediter	shipping clerk
verbalize	talk

For more examples of nontraditional English, refer to Section 49 and to Sections 42-48 in Chapter 5.

51. Use Short, Simple Words, Sentences, and Paragraphs

The recommendation to use simple language with short words, sentences, and paragraphs in the body of your letters is good advice whether you're writing to someone in the United States or in another country. (The body of a letter is described in Section 56 of Chapter 7.)

Whereas short, simple language is helpful to domestic readers, it's essential to foreign readers. The only exception occurs with the need to avoid undesirable language, such as cliches or slang, or to expand a subject to make it clearer. In such cases, as long as the message is simple and easy to comprehend, additional words may be justified.

Simplicity is the key. It won't work to try to impress foreign readers with big, complex, pretentious words and sentences.

(For more about pretentious language, refer to Section 44 in Chapter 5.) They are more likely to think you're inconsiderate than intelligent. Complexity is the enemy of anyone who has to translate a letter into another language. Even English-speaking readers hate complexity. Which of the following letters would you rather receive?

> Dear Mrs. Acktenburg:
>
> I have before me your letter requesting clarification of Clause 1.R in our contract.
>
> In regard to changes that might affect territorial rights: In the event that any territorial rights may be affected hereunder by modification of existing laws or changes in market arrangements, said changes shall not prevent the continuance of this Agreement, and appropriate adjustments in the grant of rights under Clause 1.R shall be subject to mutual agreement between the two companies.
>
> Please let me know if you have any further questions.
>
> Sincerely,

> Dear Mrs. Acktenburg:
>
> Thank you for asking about the meaning of Clause 1.R in our contract.
>
> Clause 1.R explains what happens to territorial rights if any changes occur. Territorial rights may be affected by two changes:
>
> 1. Changes in the law
>
> 2. Changes in the market plan

Such changes will not cause our contract to end. It will continue. However, our companies may mutually agree to revise the way that territorial rights are granted. Either your company or my company may propose and discuss a revision at any time.

Please telephone or write if you have any other questions. We want your company to enjoy all benefits provided by our contract.

Sincerely,

Most people would find the second version much more palatable.

Choosing Short Words

Vocabulary. If you have developed a large vocabulary for domestic use and like to make your letters more interesting by drawing on it, you may have to learn how *not* to use it or how to apply it in international correspondence. This does not mean that the variety of a large vocabulary is bad and that the monotony of a small vocabulary is good; it means that *complexity* in any form is taboo in international correspondence. A large vocabulary is generally a very useful tool, and the numerous options available with a large vocabulary can even help you to avoid complexity in your international letters.

Some writers compose domestic and international messages the same way but then return to the international messages and edit out the complexity. Whenever they see a long, complex word, they substitute a simple, short word. It doesn't matter, therefore, whether you use a simple vocabulary in the first draft or whether you return to it and substitute short, simple words in the second draft.

Word Length. A principal rule in any type of correspondence is this: When you have a choice, choose a simple, short word over a long, complicated word. After you have drafted a letter, it's easy to see differences in word length, as the previous two letters illustrate.

Word length, however, isn't always the determining factor. The word *associate*, for example, is longer than *pal*, *friend*, or *consort*, but *associate* is a more accurate designation of someone you work with in business. *Umbrage* is shorter than *dissatisfaction* or *displeasure* but is also less familiar to most readers. In general, though, look for a *suitable* short substitute for a longer, more complex word, for example: *end* (*terminate*), *delay* (*procrastinate*), *dismay* (*apprehension*), *normal* (*conventional*). Although it would be impossible to write letters in which all words have only one syllable, it is true that the fewer the syllables a word has, the shorter and simpler it will be. *Give*, for example, is shorter and simpler than the multisyllable word *contribute*.

Prefixes and Suffixes. Watch for the unnecessary addition of affixes. Both prefixes and suffixes lengthen a word and add another syllable to it. For example:

Prefixes	Suffixes
*co*exist	cancell*ation*
*non*essential	depend*ence*
*over*rate	destruct*ible*
*pre*examine	manage*ment*
*semi*circle	modif*ication*

Just as it would be difficult to use only one-syllable words in a letter, it may not always be possible or desirable to avoid all words with affixes. But some are unnecessary, as the second letter to Mr. Aoki illustrates.

Dear Mr. Aoki:

Enclosed please find the business plan you requested on the management of multidivision corporations. We hope this representation will be helpful to you in forming divisions that will operate more efficiently.

Please don't hesitate to ask if we can answer any additional questions.

Sincerely,

Dear Mr. Aoki:

Here is the business plan you requested. It explains how to manage companies with two or more divisions. We hope the plan will help you to form more efficient divisions.

Please write or telephone if you have any questions. Thank you for your interest.

Sincerely,

Choosing Short Sentences and Paragraphs

The more words a sentence has, the harder it is to read and understand. A long, complex sentence is a problem for foreign readers to translate—even when it contains primarily short, simple words. The other extreme—an incomplete sentence (sentence fragment)—is just as hard to translate as a long sentence. Skilled writers sometimes interject a sentence fragment to achieve a conversational tone, but the practice should be avoided in international correspondence. A foreign reader might puzzle endlessly over an incomplete sentence.

The same principle applies to paragraphs. Long, rambling paragraphs are hard to translate. If you want to be certain your foreign readers can easily translate and understand your letters, recast overly long sentences as two or more shorter versions. Similarly, divide long paragraphs into two or more shorter versions, or use lists and other easy-to-read features to simplify complex discussions.

Don't worry if the body of your letter sounds or looks choppy because of the short words and short sentences and paragraphs. The very act of translating something changes everything anyway. Besides, foreign readers are more concerned about ease of translation than glamorous prose.

Wordiness. Since the first objective of an international letter is clarity, not brevity, it's important not to let the goal of short, simple words, sentences, and paragraphs lead you away from using all the words needed to make yourself understood. Some words, though, are superfluous and will hinder more than help a foreign reader, as you can see in the first letter to Mr. Rimbald. The unnecessary words have been eliminated in the second letter.

> Dear Mr. Rimbald:
>
> Thank you for your letter dated July 7, 1994, asking about credit plans for businesses. Our firm has three different kinds of credit plans. All of them good ones. I'm enclosing a copy of all three of the plans for you.
>
> Needless to say, we will be happy to open an account for your company. I will be away from the office during the month of August but will be here after the first of September to help you.
>
> Please don't hesitate to let me know if you have any further questions. Thanks for your interest in Brownwell Exports, Inc.
>
> Sincerely,

> Dear Mr. Rimbald:
>
> Thank you for your July 23, 1994, letter asking about business credit plans. We have three useful plans. A copy of each one is enclosed.
>
> We would be happy to open an account for your company. I will be gone in August but will be here after September 1 to help you.

Please write or telephone if you have any questions. Thank you for your interest in Brownwell Exports.

Sincerely,

When a paragraph includes a series of items, you can simplify it by using a displayed list. The second version of the next letter follows this advice and also improves the composition.

Dear Mrs. Van Voort:

I'm pleased to hear that you're interested in the subject of hazardous-waste management. We hope your company can successfully deal with this serious problem.

My firm uses four techniques for the safe management of hazardous waste: reduction, recycling, treatment (thermal, chemical, biological), and land disposal.

The enclosed booklet explains how the various processes work. I hope this will be helpful, but please don't hesitate to let me know if you have any questions.

Sincerely,

Dear Mrs. Van Voort:

I am glad to know about your interest in ways to manage hazardous waste. I wish your company success in efforts to solve this serious problem.

My firm uses four safe methods to manage and dispose of hazardous waste:

1. Reduce the volume of hazardous waste.

2. Make new products from hazardous material.

3. Make waste less hazardous by using heat, chemicals, or microorganisms.

4. Bury the hazardous waste.

The enclosed booklet explains how the four methods work. I hope this information will help you. Please write or telephone if you have any questions.

Sincerely,

As you can see, simplifying the body of the previous letter actually lengthened rather than shortened it. The justification for doing this is that clarity is a more important goal than brevity. Sometimes clarity is best achieved through simplification, and simplification is best achieved by isolating, displaying, and spreading out certain material, such as a series of items. Nevertheless, simple, short words, sentences, and paragraphs are among the most essential elements of international correspondence.

52. OVERPUNCTUATE INTERNATIONAL MESSAGES

All messages need to be punctuated properly to help readers avoid misreading and to contribute to better and faster reader comprehension. International messages need to guide readers carefully through every sentence. The punctuation must indicate every pause and every shift in emphasis. Ideally, your message will also use simple, basic English (Chapter 5 and Sections 49 and 50 in this chapter) and short, simple words and sentences (Section 51).

Refer to Section 56 in Chapter 7 for examples of proper punctuation in the inside address, salutation, complimentary close, and other parts of international letters and memos.

Punctuation Marks

The principal marks of punctuation are the apostrophe, colon, comma, dash, ellipsis points, exclamation point, hyphen, parentheses and brackets, period, question mark, quotation marks, semicolon, and virgule (slash). Section 11 in Chapter 2 describes the use of all of these marks. Some marks are less common in international correspondence. In domestic correspondence, for example, writers sometimes use an exclamation point to signal that a remark just made is meant to be clever, funny, or facetious. But foreign readers often do not realize this.

To avoid confusing a foreign reader, use periods, commas, and other marks common to basic, straightforward English composition. Avoid exclamation points, ellipsis points (except to show omissions in quoted passages), dashes, and virgules (use a hyphen instead of a virgule: 1994-1995).

International Style

Need for Heavy Punctuation. The important difference in punctuation between domestic and international correspondence is that a heavier use of punctuation is required in international letters. In domestic correspondence, for example, you might tend to omit commas after some short introductory phrases ("in some cases") or between two very short sentences connected by a conjunction ("He arrived on Tuesday and he left the same day") but would include the commas in an international letter.

In the following example of an international message, every technically correct use of punctuation is included.

Dear Mr. Dziewanowski:

   On January 16, we sent you an order for the following items: six (6) boxes of Old World Ornaments. We enclosed our check for $60.79, along with our order 157671A (copy enclosed).

Since it is now May 16, and since the ornaments have not arrived, we wonder if our order reached you. If it did not, please tell us. We will then send another check to replace the one that was lost.

Thank you for your help.

Sincerely,

Potential Pitfalls. Although heavy punctuation is helpful to a foreign reader, the placement of the punctuation marks must be correct or the reader will be confused. It's as easy to trip over a sentence with misplaced punctuation as it is to misread a sentence with too little punctuation. You can see the difference in the next two letters, the first of which has both missing punctuation and misplaced punctuation. The second version corrects this problem.

Dear Mr. Vazquez:

We are happy that you will attend the National Forum. Your registration is confirmed and we look forward to meeting you in July.

Mrs. Charlene Steele Western, Area manager, expects many Latin American guests. Therefore she has requested rooms for guests in four hotels. We urge you to send your hotel room reservation card by June 1, 1995.

You asked about sessions on computers and electronic mail. The enclosed program includes computer technology, electronic, and voice mail.

Please write or telephone if you have any questions. We will be happy to help you complete your plans to attend the forum.

Sincerely,

Dear Mr. Vazquez:

We are happy that you will attend the National Forum. Your registration is confirmed, and we look forward to meeting you in July.

Mrs. Charlene Steele, the Western Area manager, expects many Latin American guests. Therefore, she has requested rooms for guests in four hotels. We urge you to send your hotel-room-reservation card by June 1, 1995.

You asked about sessions on computers and electronic mail. The enclosed program includes (1) computer technology and (2) electronic and voice mail.

Please write or telephone if you have any questions. We will be happy to help you complete your plans to attend the forum.

Sincerely,

Punctuation and References to Money. Punctuation in sentences referring to money must be used with great care. If you state, for example, that the price of something "has increased $2.30 to $41.75," the reader may assume that the original price was $2.30. If you insert a comma after $2.30 ("The price has increased $2.30, to $41.75"), the meaning changes. Then it means that an original price of $39.45 went up by $2.30, and the price is now $41.75. To avoid any chance of misunderstanding, recast such sentences: "The price has increased by $2.30, from $39.45 to $41.75."

Section 11 in Chapter 2 has more examples of missing and misplaced punctuation.

53. RESPECT THE READER'S CULTURE AND CUSTOMS

When you're writing a letter—domestic or foreign—you always need to be sensitive to the reader's feelings. Common sense suggests that thoughtlessness and disrespect are likely to provoke a negative attitude and response to your letters.

What You Need to Know

If you're writing to someone in the United States, you no doubt know much more about the person's culture and customs than you would know if you were writing to someone in Calcutta, India, or Shanghai, China. You may know that you shouldn't rave about the delicious steak dinner you had to a Hindu or suggest to a Buddhist that reincarnation is stupid. But do you really know enough to avoid offending someone in another country? For example:

- Do you know the proper way to address men and women, using the proper personal and professional titles, in other countries?
- Do you know which name is the family name and which is the given name of someone in a country such as Japan?
- Do you know if the person you're writing to lives in a country that frowns on American first-name casualness?
- Do you know if some topics, such as politics, sex, and religion, are taboo in the other country?
- Do you know if your reader thinks humor is inappropriate?
- Do you know if businesspeople in the other country object to conducting business before certain preliminary get-acquainted discussions?
- Do you know how the individual is viewed in relation to the organization?
- Do you know how women are considered in relation to men? Is it considered inappropriate, for example, to discuss important matters with women?

As you can see, it would be very easy to make an innocent, but irreparable, mistake if you didn't take time to study the other person's culture and customs before writing. Refer to

Sections 56 and 57 in Chapter 7 for rules about titles, names, and the proper way to address people in other countries.

Sources of Information

Nearly two hundred independent nations exist in the world, sometimes with many different cultures and customs within a single nation. If you write to people in several nations or regions within a nation, the task of learning about all the cultures and customs may seem formidable. However, a number of sources of information are available to help you.

Government and Agency Sources. The U.S. Government Printing Office in Washington, D.C., sells the list "Key Officers of Foreign Service Posts" (Publication 7877) by single copy or subscription and sells newsletter-style profiles of most countries (*Background Notes*). The Department of Commerce has a free list of numbers you can call for information about the different countries and regions of the world, and the international offices of other organizations also provide information, for example: Export-Import Bank of the United States, U.S. Department of State, U.S. Small Business Administration, and the Overseas Private Investment Corporation.

Private Sources. The Yellow Pages of your telephone directory will list schools and other organizations providing international studies or consulting services. Two schools that are well known nationally are the Business Council for International Understanding at American University in Washington, D.C., and the David M. Kennedy Center for International Studies at Brigham Young University in Provo, Utah, which sells country profiles in a newsletter-style publication (*Culturgram*). Profiles are also published in world almanacs and fact books, such as the *Information Please Almanac* (Houghton Mifflin), *The Statesman's Year-Book* (St. Martin's Press), and *The World Factbook* (Central Intelligence Agency).

Travel books, such as the *World Travel Guide* (Columbus Press), often have useful social and business information on the countries of the world. You will also find numerous books about specific countries or regions, such as *Japanese Language and Culture for Business and Travel* (University of Hawaii Press), or about international communication in general, such as *Do's and Taboos Around the World* (Wiley); especially, look for books that discuss protocol, customs, and etiquette. Other useful books are *International English Usage* (New York University Press) and *Internationally Yours: A Guide to Communicating Successfully in the Global Marketplace* (Houghton Mifflin).

Start Your Own Fact Book. Some letter writers keep a notebook or computer file in which they record useful facts about the customs and culture of their readers. The sources just mentioned have a variety of information that will help you learn what you need to know about your foreign readers. For example:

- People in Latin and South America call themselves "Americans," too, and men in this region traditionally consider themselves superior to women.
- Japanese believe that companies and groups take precedence over individuals, so it is preferable to refer to "your company" rather than "you": "Your company may be interested in this information."

For every country to which you send letters, make a list of the aspects of culture and customs that might directly or indirectly influence how your readers will respond to what you say and how you say it. You might organize this information, manually or by computer, according to topics, such as religion, language, family, government and politics, economics and finance (both personal and business), the environment, business practices, social conventions, and holidays. Until you know a country or region thoroughly, keep adding to your fact book and refer to it every time you are ready to compose an international letter.

7

Mechanics of Correspondence

54. STATIONERY

Business Stationery

Letter Stationery. Organizations choose paper and letterhead designs that reflect the image they want to project. A law firm, for example, might reflect its conservative character by choosing an off-white, smooth or lightly textured paper, with a traditional type style printed or engraved in black ink. A video store, however, might prefer a livelier appearance, with heavily textured colored paper and colored ink, as well as a bright, decorative design combining modern type and eye-catching artwork. What appears to be good taste for the law firm might be too bland or traditional for the video store, and what appears to enhance the contemporary image of the video store might seem too novel or bold for the law firm. Appropriateness, therefore, must be considered on an individual basis.

Business stationery provides the organization's name; address; telephone, fax, and other numbers; and sometimes the names of officers or executives. It may also include an emblem or other logo design officially adopted by the organization. Printers and some stationery and office-supply stores have numerous stationery samples available and can make recommendations about quality of paper, appropriate weight, suitable type styles, and other factors.

Additional pages of a letter or memo (continuation pages) should be prepared on the same paper as that used for the first page. If headings are printed on continuation pages, they may include the organization's name; address; and telephone, fax, or other numbers.

Standard business stationery is 8 1/2 by 11 inches and is folded in thirds to fit into a standard business envelope. Executives additionally may use smaller writing paper for personal or social-business messages, such as thank yous and condolences to business associates. See the description under "Social and Personal Stationery."

Memo Stationery. The same stationery used for letters may be used for memos; smaller size sheets are also appropriate for memos. Guide words, such as *Date* and *To,* may be printed at the top of the page on the sheets designated for memo usage, or they may be typed on the page along with the rest of the memo.

Social and Personal Stationery

Writing Paper. Personal writing paper may be used for both social and personal letters. Regular business stationery is used when a social-business letter is written on behalf of an organization, for example, a letter of congratulations from a supplier on the tenth company anniversary of an important customer. If an executive were sending a personal congratulatory message to a friend, however, rather than a message sent as a representative of a company or on behalf of a company, the letter should be sent on the executive's personal writing paper.

Other nonbusiness letters, such as personal letters to friends and relatives, may also be sent on personal writing paper. However, many writers use anything from a ruled pad to commercial stationery for such personal letters.

Personal writing paper for men and women may be used for both handwritten messages and nonbusiness messages prepared by typewriter or computer. Men's writing paper of about 7 1/2 by 10 1/2 inches can be folded in thirds and women's paper of about $5^{1}/_{2}$ by $7^{1}/_{2}$ inches can be folded in half to fit a small matching envelope. Consult a current etiquette book for information on the printing or engraving of personal writing paper.

Foldovers. Foldover notepaper or foldover cards (informals) of at least $3^{1}/_{2}$ by 5 inches when folded—the minimum size allowed by the U.S. Postal Service—are useful for very short messages, such as a thank you or expression of sympathy. Often the sender's initials or name is printed or engraved on the front panel of the folded sheet or card.

55. LETTER AND MEMO FORMATS

Standard Letter Formats

The most common business and social letter formats are the full-block, block, modified-block, and simplified formats. The simplified style, however, is more common in business usage. Although no standard format exists for a personal letter, it may follow any of the standard business and social layouts. But it would not include certain business parts, such as an attention line. (Section 56 describes the principal parts of letters.)

Most personal letters begin with the date, followed by an informal salutation. Many, however, omit the greeting and move directly into the body of the letter. It is always thoughtful to include your return address even in a personal letter. It should be given before the date and is usually placed in the upper right corner or centered.

The examples at the end of this section include four standard business and social formats and a common personal format. Although most personal letters are handwritten, they may be typed, as illustrated in the personal model provided in this section. Refer to Section 6 in Chapter 1 and to Section 59 in this chapter for examples of correspondence that should be handwritten or printed.

Continuation-Page Format

The format for letter or memo continuation pages—second, third, and other succeeding pages—should be the same as that for the first page. Different styles for continuation-page headings are described in Section 56.

Continuation-page headings are used in business and social letters. Personal letter writers don't use a formal continuation-page heading but, rather, put only the page number at the top of the continuation page. Business and social letters, however, require a heading that consists of the addressee's name, the date, and the page number. The continuation-page model illustrated in this section uses a stacked form.

Form-Letter Format

The format used for a business form letter is the same as that used for any other business letter. Therefore, it might be a full-block, block, modified-block, or simplified layout. The most common form-letter format, however, is the modified-block layout. The model illustrated in this section is a fill-in style form letter. The basic letter is printed or stored in the computer with blank spaces. The fill-in data are added by typewriter or computer when the letter is actually sent. Many computer programs have merge features whereby individual data, such as names and numbers, can be merged with the standard portion of the letter.

Standard Memo Format

So many different memo formats exist that it is questionable whether any one should be called a "standard" format. But many memos are prepared on regular business stationery, and certain guide words, such as *To* and *From*, are always used. Section 56 describes the principal parts of memos. The model format in this section is suitable for memo messages prepared on regular business stationery, 8 1/2 by 11 inches. For a memo continuation page, use the same format as that used for a letter continuation page.

FULL-BLOCK FORMAT

[LETTERHEAD]

March 16, 1994

Your reference OT4000

Ms. Sharon C. Stalvey
Manager, Advertising and Promotion
American Originals, Inc.
100 Marshall Lane
Stamford, CT 06904

Dear Ms. Stalvey:

LETTER FORMATTING BY COMPUTER

Thank you for requesting our new booklet
describing letter formatting by computer. A
complimentary copy is enclosed.

This letter has been prepared in the modern full-
block format. Because it permits easy setup, it
is one of the most popular formats in use today.

If you have any questions, Ms. Stalvey, please let
me know. We appreciate your interest in our
formatting guidelines.

Sincerely,

Arnold K. Dexter
Manager

lks

Enc.

BLOCK FORMAT

[LETTERHEAD]

March 16, 1994

Porter Communications, Inc.
200 Billings Avenue, N.W.
Mason, UT 84622

Attention Dr. Henry P. Jenkins, Manager

Ladies and Gentlemen:

Thank you for requesting our new booklet
describing letter formatting by computer. A
complimentary copy is enclosed.

This letter, prepared in the block format, is a
compromise between modern and traditional layouts.
It combines features of both the full-block and
modified-block layouts.

If I can answer any questions, please let me know.
We appreciate Porter Communications' interest in
our formatting guidelines.

Sincerely,

Arnold K. Dexter
Manager

lks

Enc.

MODIFIED-BLOCK FORMAT

[LETTERHEAD]

March 16, 1994

Mr. Adam J. Shapiro
G. T. Gold & Sons
300 Pendleton Lane
Boston, MA 02115

Dear Mr. Shapiro:

Thank you for requesting our new booklet
describing letter formatting by computer. A
complimentary copy is enclosed.

This letter has been prepared in a
traditional modified-block format. The oldest
business format, this layout is often preferred by
conservative organizations.

If you have any questions, Mr. Shapiro,
please let me know. We appreciate your interest
in our formatting guidelines.

Sincerely,

Arnold K. Dexter
Manager

lks

Enc.

P.S. I'm also enclosing a copy of our
<u>Computer Accessories Catalog</u>, which contains other
items that may be of interest to you. AKD

SIMPLIFIED FORMAT

[LETTERHEAD]

March 16, 1994

Ms. Marlene D. Hopkins, Manager
Word Processing Department
Festive Greeting Cards
P.O. Box 2000
Hanover, PA 17333

WORD PROCESSING SKILLS

Thank you, Ms. Hopkins, for asking about ways to
improve word processing skills. I am enclosing a
complimentary copy of our new booklet describing
letter formatting by computer.

This letter has been prepared in the simplified
format. This layout is a modern form preferred by
many word processing operators.

If you have any questions, Ms. Hopkins, please let
me know. We appreciate your interest in
guidelines that promote better word processing
skills.

Arnold K. Dexter
Manager

lks

Enc.

PERSONAL FORMAT

300 Maple Drive
Cleveland, OH 44127

April 1, 1994

Hi, Marge,

Jed and I were talking about you and Ken this morning. Don't worry--it was all good!

Do you realize it has been almost a year since we've seen each other? It was Easter weekend last year--which leads me to the reason for this letter (you thought it was to wish you Happy April Fool's Day, didn't you?): Could you, Ken, and the kids come to our house for a visit over Easter weekend this year? Friday to Monday would be great if Ken can get off work that long. But I'll settle for whatever you can manage.

We'd really love to see all of you, so I desperately hope you can come. If another time is better, though, let me know. I'm sure we can work out something, and it will be <u>such fun</u>!

I'll save other news till we see all of you. Take care.

Love from all of us,

CONTINUATION-PAGE FORMAT

[CONTINUATION-PAGE RETURN ADDRESS (OPTIONAL)]

Marlene D. Hopkins
March 16, 1994
page two

format.   This layout is a modern form preferred by
many word processing operators.

If you have any questions, Ms. Hopkins, please let
me know.   We appreciate your interest in
guidelines that promote better word processing
skills.

Arnold K. Dexter
Manager

lks

Enc.

FILL-IN FORM-LETTER FORMAT

[LETTERHEAD]

Dear

      Just a friendly reminder that your payment
of   due on   has not yet
arrived.

      If your check is already in the mail, please
disregard this notice and accept our thanks. If
it is not, won't you please take a moment to mail
it today?

                      Cordially,

                      Eldon V. Fennister
                      Credit Manager

STANDARD MEMO FORMAT

[LETTERHEAD]

DATE: May 7, 1994

TO: Shipping Department

FROM: Harold M. Weiland, Jr.

SUBJECT: Ordering Information

On May 21, Schaefer Telecom will complete the installation of new telephone and facsimile equipment throughout our company. As a result of this modernization, the following changes will affect customer-ordering procedures.

Effective May 21 customers will have two options for placing orders in addition to conventional mail-order practices:

1. Customers may place toll-free telephone orders by calling 1-800-555-6161, twenty-four hours a day, seven days a week.

2. Customers who prefer may also fax their orders to 1-212-555-6162.

The new summer catalog will reflect these changes. Please revise your order-fulfillment procedure to incorporate these changes.

I'll be happy to answer any questions you have about the new equipment. In the meantime, thank you very much for your help and cooperation in making our system more effective.

jg

56. PRINCIPAL PARTS OF LETTERS AND MEMOS

Parts of Business, Social, and Personal Letters

Business Letters. A business letter often has more parts than a social or personal letter has. It may include some or all of the following parts: date, reference line, confidential notation, inside address, attention line, salutation, body, complimentary close, signature, identification line, enclosure notation, mail notation, copy notation, and postscript. Some parts, such as the postscript, are not used at all or are used less frequently in international correspondence.

Social and Personal Letters. Social and personal letters may have some or all of the following parts: date, inside address, salutation, body, complimentary close, signature, and postscript. Refer to Section 55 for examples of formats that incorporate some of these parts, to Section 58 for common envelope formats, and to Section 54 for information on business, social, and personal stationery.

Date

The first part of a letter, after any printed or typed return address, is usually the date.

Format. Place the date against the left margin in the full-block and simplified formats and a little to the right of the center of the page in the block and modified-block formats. Begin the date two to four line spaces beneath the printed letterhead address or typed return address. If you don't include a return address on your personal stationery in letters sent to close friends and relatives, begin the date about 1 ½ inches below the top edge of the paper. (Although friends and relatives may either know your address or have it available, it is always thoughtful to include it on your letters so that they don't have to search for it.)

Standard Order. To avoid confusion, always spell out the month. In some countries, for example, 9/8/95 means August 9, 1995. To most people in the United States, it means

September 8, 1995, but it could be misinterpreted by someone unfamiliar with this form of shorthand. The standard order in general business, social, and personal letters is month, day, and year: *September 8, 1995*; in the military services the order is day, month, and year, with no commas: *8 September 1995*.

Reference Line

A reference line is used only in a business letter, where it designates the file number of the correspondence or the code for the matter being discussed.

Format. Place the reference two line spaces beneath the date, aligned at the left under the first word of the date.

If your business letterhead has a printed line, however, such as "In reply please refer to," insert your own file reference immediately after that printed line, regardless of where it may be on the page. Then, place the reference (if any) of the addressee on the next line. Spell out the word *Reference* in international correspondence (unless it is already printed on your stationery in abbreviated form). The following examples are three common styles for writing reference lines and positioning it in conjunction with the date.

Reader's reference line only:

```
September 8, 1995

Your reference EK-1234
```

Both reader's and sender's reference line:

```
September 8, 1995

Our reference KE-4321
Your reference EK-1234
```

With printed reference line:

When replying, refer to: KE-4321
Your reference EK-1234

September 8, 1995

Confidential Notation

Including a confidential notation on the envelope means that you don't want anyone but the addressee to open it. The notation is sometimes used in a private letter sent to a business address where envelopes might be opened by a secretary or mail room clerk.

Format. Place the confidential notation against the left margin in all formats, about two line spaces below the date or reference line. Write the notation in all capital letters or underlined with an initial capital.

CONFIDENTIAL

Confidential

Inside Address

The name and address data on the envelope and the letter are usually identical. Sometimes, however, certain nonaddress account data are added to the envelope, or an all-capitals format without punctuation is used on the envelope for postal optical-character reading machines. Refer to the information on envelope addressing in this section and in Section 58.

Occasionally, an envelope is addressed to a company, whereas the inside address on the letter specifies an individual. This is done when the writer wants the envelope to be opened and the letter read even if the addressee is away. The next section discusses the more common option of using an attention line in such cases.

Format. Single-space the inside address, and place it against the left margin in all formats. Writers frequently omit the inside address in personal letters to close friends and relatives. Depending on the size of the letter, the inside address may be positioned from two to twelve line spaces below the date or reference line.

Titles and Names. Use the proper personal or professional title preceding the addressee's name, as described in Section 57. That discussion also provides guidelines on using scholastic degrees and other initials after a name and in conjunction with other titles preceding the name.

If a job title is included in the inside address, place it on the same line as the name if it is short; otherwise put it on a line immediately below the name. Although the name of a department in a company traditionally appears on a line after the company's name, if it is short it may be included with the addressee's job title on the line immediately after the addressee's name.

Mr. Edmund C. Guarani, Manager
Hendricks Electronics, Inc.
Purchasing Department
10 New Street
Princeton, NJ 08540

Mr. Edmund C. Guarani
Manager, Purchasing Department
Hendricks Electronics, Inc.
10 New Street
Princeton, NJ 08540

Mr. Edmund C. Guarani
Manager, New Product Development
Hendricks Electronics, Inc.
Design and Engineering Department
10 New Street
Princeton, NJ 08540

Omit the job title and company name in a social or personal letter written to someone at home.

Mr. Edmund C. Guarani
19 Maple Drive
Princeton, NJ 08540

Two or More Addressees. If a letter is sent to two or more people, stack the names, with the person of highest rank listed first. If both people hold equal positions, list the names in alphabetical order.

Mr. Edmund C. Guarani, Manager
Ms. Loretta Ostermeyer, Supervisor
Hendricks Electronics, Inc.
Purchasing Department
10 New Street
Princeton, NJ 08540

Room Numbers. Room numbers, apartment numbers, or floor numbers are traditionally stated after the street address, after a department or building name, or on a separate line after these elements or beneath the person's name.

Mr. Edmund C. Guarani
19 Maple Drive, Apt. 2F
Princeton, NJ 08540

Mr. Edmund C. Guarani
Hendricks Electronics, Inc.
Hendricks Building, Room 42
10 New Street
Princeton, NJ 08540

In Care of. If a letter is sent in care of another person, place that person's name on the line immediately below the addressee's name, preceded by the abbreviation *c/o* or the words *In care of.*

> Mr. Edmund C. Guarani
> c/o Thomas R. Herter

> Mr. Edmund C. Guarani
> In care of Thomas R. Herter

Foreign Addresses. In a foreign address, include the country name on the last line of the inside address in all capitals or on the same line as the city. The country must be on the last line alone on the envelope.

> Ms. Sharon Leilat, President
> Ontario Industries Ltd.
> 100 Marketplace Boulevard
> Ottawa ON K1A OB1
> CANADA

> Ms. Sharon Leilat, President
> Ontario Industries Ltd.
> 100 Marketplace Boulevard
> Ottawa ON K1A OB1, Canada

Company-Name Style. In writing the name of a company, follow the organization's style of capitalizing and punctuating its name and abbreviating or spelling out the words *Company* (*Co.*) and *Corporation* (*Corp.*). Use or omit a comma before the abbreviations *Inc.* and *Ltd.* according to the organization's official style.

Street Address Style. In the street address, spell out only the number one designating a house or building number (*One West Avenue*), and spell out *one* through *ten* in street names; use numerals above ten (*1040 Third Avenue, 1040 North 22d Street* or *1040 North 22 Street*). Use *th, st,* and *d* after a number when necessary to avoid confusing the house or building numbers with the street numbers (*16 34th Street,* not *16 34*

Street). Abbreviate compound directions following a street if they designate part of a city (*100 Wildwood Lane, NW*), but spell out compass points that are part of a street name (*200 Palm Boulevard South*). Also, spell out *Street, Boulevard,* and other key words in the street name.

A post office box number may be used in place of a street address. Some individuals and companies include both on their stationery. If you copy both the street and box number onto the envelope, it will be delivered to the one that you list last. In the next example, the letter will go to the box number. Use the zip code that applies to whichever location is listed last, the street or box number.

> Mr. Edmund C. Guarani
> 19 Maple Drive
> P.O. Box 600, Central Station
> Princeton, NJ 08540

State and Zip Code Style. Use the two-letter postal abbreviation for states followed by the associated zip code. Include the additional four-digit code when known: *Princeton, NJ 08540-1234.*

Carryover Lines. If a very long line in the inside address runs over to the next line, indent the carryover line a quarter to a half inch.

> Mr. Edmund C. Guarani
> Manager, New Products Design,
>   Development, and Testing
> Hendricks Electronics, Inc.

Attention Line

Attention lines are used primarily in domestic business correspondence to be certain that a letter is opened and acted upon. If the letter is addressed to a company, with an attention line to an individual, the letter will be opened even if the person named in the attention line is absent. If the letter is addressed to an individual, with an attention line to another person, it will go to the person in the attention line if the addressee is absent.

Format. Place the attention line against the left margin in all formats, two line spaces below the inside address. Do not punctuate or underline the attention line, but do spell out and capitalize the word *Attention*. Always use the person's full name, if known; otherwise use a title, such as *Mr.* or *Ms.* with the person's last name. (In the third example below, the person's first name is unknown.) If the person works in a large organization, include a position title or department.

```
Hendricks Electronics, Inc.
Purchasing Department
10 New Street
Princeton, NJ 08540

Attention Edmund Guarani, Manager


Mr. Edmund C. Guarani, Manager
Hendricks Electronics, Inc.
Purchasing Department
10 New Street
Princeton, NJ 08540

Attention Anita M. Feldstein, Assistant Manager


Mr. Edmund C. Guarani, Manager
Hendricks Electronics, Inc.
Purchasing Department
10 New Street
Princeton, NJ 08540

Attention Ms. Feldstein, Assistant Manager
```

Salutation

The salutation is the greeting to the addressee used in all letters—business, social, and personal.

Format. Place the salutation against the left margin in all formats. Begin two line spaces below the inside address or attention line. Put a colon after the salutation in social and business letters; a comma, in personal letters.

Dear Mr. Guarani:
Dear Dad,

Salutations to Individuals. Social and business salutations to individuals usually begin with the word *Dear.* Greetings in a personal letter could be anything from *Dear Aunt Mabel* to *Hi there.* Writers always address close friends and relatives by their first names and, when appropriate, a title, such as *Uncle,* showing the relationship. In social and business letters, the use of first names depends on the relationship of the writer and the addressee. When you're uncertain whether it's appropriate to call someone by his or her first name, use a title and the last name until asked to use the first name: *Dear Ms. Adams.* If Ms. Adams wants you to call her by her first name, she'll tell you or will sign her letter with only her first name. If she signs with her full name, it's a clue that she wants you to continue calling her "Ms. Adams."

When you know the addressee's name, gender, and personal or professional title, follow the standard form for a salutation: *Dear Captain McKenzie.* If you don't know the addressee's name or gender but do know the person's title, use the title alone for the salutation: *Dear Editor.* If you know the person's name but not the gender, use the first name in place of a title such as *Mr.: Dear Leslie Acktenburg.* If you don't know the name, gender, or title, use *Dear Sir or Madam* or address the letter generally to the company.

No title or other designation should be used after a name in the salutation: *Dear Mrs. Rogers* (not *Dear Mrs. Rogers, Treasurer*). But a personal, professional, or honorary title should precede the last name when known: *Dear Major Vadim.* Only a few dignitaries, such as the president of the United States, are addressed by title only, even when the name is known: *Dear Mr. President.*

The salutation to two or more people should include the same personal, professional, or honorary titles used in the inside address.

> Mr. Edmund C. Guarani, Manager
> Ms. Loretta Ostermeyer, Supervisor
> Hendricks Electronics, Inc.
> Purchasing Department
> 10 New Street
> Princeton, NJ 08540
>
> Dear Mr. Guarani and Ms. Ostermeyer:

Follow the guidelines in Section 57 for addressing a married couple when one is titled and the other is not.

In a few countries, titles such as *Lawyer* and *Engineer* are used with the addressee's name, but in most countries, the common titles are *Dr.*, *Mr.*, *Mrs.*, or *Miss*. The title *Ms.* is not common in other countries, and in international correspondence, addressees should not be addressed by that title; however, if you want your foreign contacts to address you as *Ms.*, put that title in parentheses before your name in the typed signature line of your letter.

If you are writing to someone with an unfamiliar name, ask for assistance if you have any doubts. In some countries, for example, the last-stated name is actually the person's first name, as described in Section 57.

To Whom It May Concern. If your letter is not addressed to any particular person or company, use the greeting *To Whom It May Concern* followed by a colon. Since the letter is not addressed to a particular person or organization, there can be no inside address, but the date should be positioned in the usual place below the letterhead address, and the salutation should begin about the same number of lines below the date that it would begin if an inside address had been used. Letters of recommendation or introduction are sometimes prepared with this type of impersonal salutation so that they can be copied and distributed later to anyone in any organization.

Salutations to Companies. The common salutations to a company are *Ladies and Gentlemen* if you don't know the ownership or if the ownership consists of both men and women; *Ladies*, if the ownership is women only; *Gentlemen*, if the ownership is men only.

When a letter is addressed to a company but includes an attention line to an individual, the greeting must nevertheless be to the company.

> Olson Lighting Ltd.
> 100 South Parkway
> Cleveland, OH 44127-5899
>
> Attention Ernest O. Woodward
>
> Ladies and Gentlemen:

Subject Line

A subject line is used in business correspondence to summarize the content of a letter in a few words.

Format. Place the subject against the left margin or indent it, consistent with the paragraph style of the letter—flush left or indented. Begin the subject line two line spaces below the salutation.

Writing Style. You may introduce the subject line with the word *Subject* or omit it. If used, the word *Subject* may be written in all capital letters or with an initial capital only. It is always followed by a colon. (Lawyers and certain other professionals use the phrase *In re* to begin the subject line instead of the word *Subject*, and they place it above, rather than below, the salutation.) The subject line may be underlined if desired; in any case, important words should be capitalized. Make the subject line as brief as possible, summarizing the main topic of the letter in a few words. The following styles are all acceptable.

DISK STORAGE CENTER
Disk Storage Center
Disk Storage Center
SUBJECT: DISK STORAGE CENTER
SUBJECT: Disk Storage Center
Subject: Disk Storage Center

Body

The body of the letter is the text—your message or discussion. It should be written in normal prose style, observing the rules of proper grammar, spelling, capitalization, and punctuation, as described in Chapter 2.

Format. Start your message two line spaces below the salutation or subject line. Single-space the text and put one line space between paragraphs. Leave margins on all sides of $1\frac{1}{4}$ to 2 inches, depending on the size of the letter. Indent paragraphs $\frac{1}{2}$ to 1 inch in the modified-block format and, if desired, in the personal format. In all other formats, begin paragraphs against the left margin.

Writing Style. Avoid long, cumbersome sentences and paragraphs. Use numbered lists, indented (blocked) examples, tables, or anything else that will simplify complex textual matter, especially for a foreign reader. (Refer to Section 32 for more about using a clear, simple style; refer to Section 51 in Chapter 6 for more about writing international messages.) If the letter is too long for one page, carry over at least two lines of the body to the next page.

Complimentary Close

The complimentary close is a polite way of signing off a letter, signifying that your discussion is finished.

Format. Place the complimentary close two line spaces below the body against the left margin in the full-block and simplified formats—and, if desired, in the personal format—and a little to the right of the center of the page in all other formats. Capitalize only the first word of the close, and place a comma after the last word.

Common Closes. The trend in domestic correspondence is to use a warm, friendly close in business and social letters.

Sincerely,	Best regards,
Cordially,	Best wishes,
Regards,	All the best,

Use an impersonal close, such as *Sincerely,* rather than a personal close, such as *Best wishes,* to a company.

Use a formal close when writing to a high official or other prominent person.

Yours very truly,	Very sincerely yours,
Yours truly,	Respectfully,
Very truly yours,	Respectfully yours,

In international correspondence, unlike most domestic correspondence, the more formal, less familiar closings are preferred since some foreign readers are often offended by too much familiarity.

Sincerely,	Respectfully, *(very formal)*
Sincerely yours,	Respectfully yours,
Very sincerely yours,	*(very formal)*

The close used in personal letters depends on your relationship with the addressee. Letters to friends and relatives often close with a personal expression of affection.

Love,	Your friend,
With love,	Your pal,
Lots of love,	Yours,
Fondly,	Faithfully,
Affectionately,	As ever,
Warmly,	Always,

Signature

The signature in business letters consists of two or more lines: a typed company name (less common), the individual's handwritten signature, the individual's typed signature, and sometimes the individual's job title. Some executives have their name and job title printed at the top of the letter, and it is unnecessary to repeat this information in the typed signature section. A company name is included in the signature section only when the letter represents an important opinion of the firm or a contract involving the firm.

A social letter would have only two lines: the handwritten signature and the typed signature. A personal letter to close friends and relatives usually has only a handwritten signature, without any typed lines.

Format. The various lines of the signature section are placed immediately after the complimentary close. Place the individual's typed signature line four to five line spaces below the complimentary close. Place a short title immediately after your typed name, but place a long title on the line below your name. If a company name is included, place it two line spaces after the complimentary close and the typed signature line four to five line spaces after the company name. The various lines of the signature are aligned below the complimentary close, which may be against the left margin or may begin a little to the right of the center of the page.

Names and Titles. Type your name precisely as you sign it. For example, if you type the name as "Robert A. Henderson," don't sign it as "R. A. Henderson." If you sign only your first name, though, it is permissible to use a nickname or other variation from the typed name.

The way you sign your name tells the reader what you want to be called. If you sign only your first name, it indicates that you want to be on a first-name basis; if you sign your full name, it indicates that you want to be addressed by a title and your last name. If you receive a letter from someone who has signed with his or her first name, it is considered courteous to reciprocate and sign your letter with your first name.

Unless you need to clarify gender, don't put the title *Mr.* or *Ms.* in parentheses before your typed name in domestic correspondence. But do put the title *Mrs.* in parentheses before your typed name if you want to be addressed that way. Otherwise the recipient will assume that a woman wants to be addressed as *Ms.* In international letters, you must also put *Ms.* in parentheses in front of your name if you want to be addressed that way. Foreign readers are unfamiliar with that title and would probably address you as *Miss* or *Mrs.* if you omitted it. Academic degrees, if used, should be placed after the typed name. The handwritten signature, however, should not include either titles or degrees.

Current Forms. The following examples of various typed signature lines and their position below the complimentary close illustrate the correct form for men, women, companies, and secretaries. The examples that include job titles are suitable only for business correspondence. Most of the other forms may be used in both business and social letters. If an example is suitable for very formal social situations, that explanation appears in brackets next to the example.

Anyone replying to a letter will use the name and title that you put in your signature line. Therefore, if you prefer *William Symington*, don't type *W. H. Symington* in the signature line. If you want to be addressed as *Mrs. Joan D. Branson*, rather than *Ms. Joan D. Branson*, don't forget to put *Mrs.* in parentheses before your name in the typed signature line.

Men:

Sincerely,

John H. Sax

John H. Sax, Dean

Sincerely,

J. H. Sax

(Mr.) J. H. Sax

Sincerely,

John H. Sax Sr.

John H. Sax Sr.
Personnel Director

Sincerely,

John H. Sax III

John H. Sax III, M.D.

Single women:

Sincerely,

Nancy S. Booker

Nancy S. Booker

Sincerely,

N. S. Booker

(Ms.) N. S. Booker

Sincerely,

Nancy S. Booker

Nancy S. Booker
Executive Assistant

Sincerely,

Nancy S. Booker

Nancy S. Booker, CPA

Married and widowed women:

Sincerely,

Joan D. Hewitt

Joan D. Hewitt

Sincerely,

Joan Deming Hewitt

Joan Deming Hewitt

Sincerely,

Joan Deming

Joan Deming

Sincerely,

Joan D. Hewitt

(Mrs.) Joan D. Hewitt

Sincerely,

J. D. Hewitt

(Ms.) J. D. Hewitt

Sincerely,

Joan D. Hewitt

Joan D. Hewitt
Sales Manager

Sincerely, [*formal social*]

Joan D. Hewitt

(Mrs. Jake E. Hewitt)

Divorced women:

Sincerely,

Alma Bush

Alma Bush

Sincerely,

A. M. Bush

(Ms.) A. M. Bush

Sincerely,

Alma B. Hill

Alma B. Hill

Sincerely,

Alma B. Hill

(Mrs.) Alma B. Hill

Sincerely,

Alma Bush Hill

Alma Bush Hill

Sincerely,

Alma Bush Hill

(Mrs.) Alma Bush Hill

Sincerely,   [*formal social
modern*]

Alma B. Hill

(Mrs.) Alma B. Hill

Sincerely,   [*formal social
traditional*]

Alma Bush Hill

(Mrs. Bush Hill)

Companies:

Sincerely,

THE ACCOUNTING SOURCE

Orville C. Ecover

Orville C. Ecover
Director, New Accounts

Sincerely,

MILES AND WEBBER, INC.

Nora G. Weleda

Nora G. Weleda, LL.D.
Vice President

Secretaries:

Sincerely,

Sara Findlay

Sara Findlay
Secretary to Mrs. Creighton

Although the preceding example includes the secretary's name, a secretary should not type his or her own name in the signature line without permission. If not authorized to include it, the secretary should type only the employer's personal title and last name after the words *Secretary to*. But the secretary would sign his or her full name the same as would be done in any other letter.

If the secretary were actually signing the employer's name in the employer's absence, the typed name in the signature line would be that of the employer. The secretary would then hand-write "Edna A. Creighton" just above the typed name and add his or her own handwritten initials directly under the employer's handwritten last name.

Sincerely,

Edna A. Creighton
                  sf
(Mrs.) Edna A. Creighton

If the person who signs for the boss is not the secretary, the following forms are common.

Sincerely,   Sincerely,

Jeffrey R. West   *Edna A. Creighton*
                                                    JRW
For Mrs. Edna A. Creighton   (Mrs.) Edna A. Creighton

Identification Line

The identification line indicates who wrote or dictated, who signed, and who transcribed or typed a business letter. The person composing the letter and the person signing it are usually the same. Sometimes, however, assistants or others draft a letter for their employers to sign. Then three people, including the typist, are involved.

Format. Place the identification line against the left margin in all formats. Begin two line spaces below the last line of the typed signature section. Some firms omit the identification information on the original and place it only on the office copies.

Writing Style. Three sets of initials are given if the person dictating or writing the letter and the one signing it are different. If the writer is also the signer, the writer's initials are not necessary since the signer's name appears in the signature line. Follow the firm's policy in omitting or including the signer's initials. Place a colon between each set of initials without any space before or after the colon. Use all capitals for the writer and the signer and small letters for the typist.

Style	Example
Writer, signer, and typist	EBC:MF:gr
Writer and typist	EBC:gr
Typist	gr (firm believes signer's initials are unnecessary)

If the writer's name is not used in the signature line, put the writer's first and middle initials and last name before the typist's initials: *EBCollins:gr*.

Enclosure Notation

In business correspondence, an enclosure notation tells the addressee what you are enclosing in the envelope along with your letter.

Format. Place the notation against the left margin in all formats, one or two line spaces below the identification line. In a long letter, all of the concluding notations—from the identification line to the copy notation—may be single-spaced. If a letter is brief, there should be enough room to double-space the various notations.

Writing Style. Depending on the number of enclosures, use *Enclosure* (*Enc.*) or *Enclosures* (*Encs.*). Spell out *Enclosure* in letters sent to non-English-speaking countries where the abbreviation *Enc.* might not be understood. If you want to be certain that the addressee doesn't overlook anything enclosed in the letter, specify after the notation exactly what is enclosed or how many items are enclosed. Also, indicate if you want any item to be returned.

Enclosure	Enclosures
Enc.	Encs.
Enc. 1	Enclosures: 2
Enc.: Check	Enclosures: Chart [*please return*]
	Address list

Mail Notation

In business correspondence, the mail notation indicates how the letter was sent if it was mailed some way other than by regular first-class postal mail. Often this information is placed only on the sender's file copy.

Format. Place the notation against the left margin in all formats. Position it one or two line spaces below the enclosure notation. (Either single-space all notations or double-space all of them.)

By registered mail
By Express Mail International Service

Copy Notation

In business correspondence, the copy notation specifies who will receive a copy of the letter besides the addressee.

Format. Place the copy notation against the left margin in all formats. Position it one or two line spaces below the mail notation, depending on whether the other notations are being single- or double-spaced.

Writing Style. The copy notation may be abbreviated or spelled out in domestic correspondence. But it should be spelled out in international correspondence since not all foreign readers know what this abbreviation means.

In domestic correspondence, a variety of copy notations is used, the most familiar being *Copy* and *c*, which refer to any type of copy, except a blind copy. Other abbreviations are *pc*, which refers to a photocopy; *cc*, which refers to a computer copy; *fc*, which refers to a fax copy; and *bc*, which refers to a blind copy. A blind copy is sent to someone without the addressee's knowledge; hence the notation *bc* should appear only on the sender's file copies and on the blind-copy recipient's copy.

```
c: Richard Bendel
pc: Richard Bendel
cc: Richard Bendel
fc: Richard Bendel
bc: Roy Glover
Copy: Richard Bendel
Copies: Richard Bendel
        Roy Glover
```

Postscript

A postscript is a brief, one- or two-sentence comment that pertains to something other than the topic discussed in the body of the letter—something that would be inappropriate in the body. It should never be something that a writer forgot to mention in the body and puts in a postscript to avoid retyping the letter. Do not use postscripts in international correspondence since non-English-speaking readers may not understand its use or the meaning of the abbreviation *P.S.*

Format. Place the postscript against the left margin or indented, depending on the paragraph style you use in the letter—flush left or indented. Position it two line spaces below the last notation of your letter in business correspondence. Add your initials immediately after the last word of the postscript. In personal correspondence, place the post-script two to four lines below the handwritten signature. The concluding initials of the postscript are omitted in personal correspondence.

> P.S. Thanks for the new sales guides. I know they
> will be a big help. RKP

Continuation-Page Heading

Most writers try to limit their letters to one page, but when a letter runs over to an additional page, a continuation-page heading is needed in social and business correspondence. Personal letter writers usually put only the page number at the top center of the next page, without a formal continuation-page heading. See Section 55 for a discussion of continuation pages and a model of such a page.

Format. Place the continuation-page heading three to four line spaces after any printed continuation-page company name and address. If printed continuation pages are not available, use a blank sheet of paper that matches the letter-head stationery, and begin the heading four to six line spaces from the top of that sheet. The word *continued* is not needed on either the first page or the continued page.

Heading. The heading in a business letter's continuation page—addressee's name, the date, and the page number—may be stacked one item under another; may be arranged in a single line beginning against the left margin, with each item separated by commas; or may be centered across the page, without commas between items and with the addressee's name against the left margin, the page number against the right margin, and the date centered in between those two items. The addressee's name may include his or her title or omit it. Both the first and last name should be included, with or without the person's title.

Ms. Stacy Larsen
November 5, 1994
page two

Stacy Larsen, November 5, 1994, page two

Stacy Larsen   November 5, 1994   page 2

Envelope

Correspondence that is sent by fax, E-mail, or another fast-messaging process does not need an envelope.Correspondence delivered through an interoffice mail system is usually sent in special interoffice company envelopes. All other mail must be properly addressed and sent through the U.S. Postal Service or a private mail-transport service. In either case, an envelope or mailing label must consist of the same information provided in the inside address of the letter. The envelope address may also include nonaddress information, such as an account number.

Format. Mail that is sent through the U.S. Postal Service to be read by optical-character reading (OCR) equipment must follow more precise specifications than mail addressed in a traditional format. (The traditional format is the most common format for personal and social correspondence, and a lot of business mail is also addressed conventionally.) The address block for OCR mail must be at least $1/2$ inch from the left and right edges of the envelope and at least $5/8$ inch from the bottom edge, with the first line no more than $2\,3/4$ inches from the bottom edge. Unit numbers, such as a room, must be placed immediately after the street on the same line, and station names must be placed right after the box number. Account numbers and other nonaddress data must be placed immediately above the first line of the address block (the addressee's name).

OCR Writing Style. The entire address must be written in all capital letters, without punctuation. (Refer to the *Domestic Mail Manual* and the *International Mail Manual* of the U.S. Postal Service for further details.) Section 58 illustrates both a traditional and an OCR envelope format.

Parts of Memos

Principal Parts in Standard Memos. Memos are used in business for interoffice correspondence; for external correspondence with associates, customers, and clients who have a friendly, close working relationship; and for electronic transmissions, such as E-mail. Although commercial formats vary widely in paper size and in the arrangement of key parts on the page, standard formats have some or all of the following parts: date, reference line, addressee line(s), sender line(s), attention line, subject line, body, signature line, identification line, enclosure notation, mail notation, copy notation, and postscript.

Memos contain a guide word, *To*, that introduces the addressee. They do not have an inside address like a traditional letter. Although some form of signature line, usually only initials, may be used in a memo, the complimentary close is omitted. The salutation is also omitted, and a confidential notation, although permissible, is often not practical since memos are frequently sent in unsealed interoffice envelopes or through an electronic system that may be accessed by others.

Section 55 includes a model of a familiar memo format. Users can purchase printed commercial memos or have their own memo stationery designed to suit their own correspondence needs. Various guide words, such as *Date* and *Subject*, are printed at the top of a memo page, and the appropriate information for each guide word is filled in later by computer or typewriter. If printed memo stationery is not available, the guide words can easily be typed on a page of regular business stationery. Refer to Section 54 for a description of memo stationery.

Date

The date in a memo is written the same as it is written in a letter: *September 8, 1995.*

Format. A guide word, *Date*, is usually printed or typed at the top left or right side of the page. Fill in the date immediately after the guide word. If a colon follows the guide word *Date*, leave one or two character spaces before filling in the date. Use consistent spacing after all guide words before filling in the appropriate information, or if you prefer, align all fill-in data on the left (see the sample memos in the appendix).

Reference Line

Like the reference line of a letter, the reference line of a memo identifies a file or other locator number.

Format. A guide word, such as *Reference*, or an abbreviation, such as *Ref.*, may be printed on a line following the *Date* line on either the left or the right side of the paper. If no such guide word is printed on the stationery, type a new guide word about two line spaces below the last of the other printed guide words. (Use the same spacing between all guide words.) Leave at least one or two character spaces after the guide word or any punctuation that follows it, such as a colon, and fill in the appropriate reference number: **REF.:** *M1-AC43.*

If you have a reference number to list and the addressee also has a number that you need to list, type two guide words, adding the words *Our* and *Your*: *Our Reference* (or *Our Ref.*) and *Your Reference* (or *Your Ref.*) Since memos are used primarily in domestic correspondence, abbreviated versions of guide words may be used. In international correspondence, however, abbreviations of any kind should be avoided.

Use a consistent punctuation style, and put colons after the typed guide words if the other printed guide words have colons following them. Also, if you are typing a guide word for the reference, follow the capitalization style of the other guide words. If abbreviated guide words are used, the period may be omitted after the abbreviations if desired: **OUR REF:** *AB-8765*. However, abbreviations in other parts of a memo should be punctuated normally.

> **OUR REF:** AB-8765
> **YOUR REF:** BA-5678

Addressee Line

The addressee line of a memo takes the place of the inside address of a letter.

Format. The addressee's name and, possibly, the address are filled in after the guide word *To.* This guide word usually appears on the left side of the paper, although the position may vary, depending on the format used. If you don't have printed memo stationery, type the word *To* on regular business stationery. Follow the same capitalization, punctuation, and spacing style used for the other guide words. Leave at least one or two character spaces after the guide word and the colon (if any) before filling in the addressee's name. The memo format may provide room only for the addressee's name or for both the addressee's name and his or her full address.

Names and Addresses. Titles may be used or omitted before the addressee's name in a memo, but the person's full name should be given. If the memo format provides room for the person's address also, follow the same style recommended for the inside address of a letter.

> **TO:** Philip Ferenc
> Manager, Sales Department
> Citrus Distributors, Inc.
> P.O. Box 2000
> Minneapolis, MN 55429-0900

Sender Line

The sender line of a memo gives the same information as the typed signature line of a traditional letter.

Format. The sender's name and, possibly, job title and department are filled in after the guide word *From*. It often appears immediately below the addressee line (*To*) but may be positioned adjacent to the addressee line on the right side of the paper, depending on the format used. If you do not have printed memo stationery, type the word *From* on regular business stationery. Follow the same capitalization, punctuation, and spacing style used for the other guide words. Leave at least one or two character spaces after the guide word and the colon (if any) before filling in the sender's name.

Use the sender's full name, but omit the personal, professional, or honorary title if it was omitted for the addressee. People who want to include their preferences may choose to use titles for both addressee and sender. If a job title is included, place a short title after the name and a long title on the next line below the name. Since the space after guide words may be very limited, words may be abbreviated to make them fit such limited space when necessary.

> **FROM:** Julia Casa-Stowe
> VP, Advertising and Prom.

Attention Line

An attention line in a memo serves the same purpose as an attention line in a letter: to insure that an envelope will be opened and the letter read even if the addressee is absent. An attention line may be used whether the addressee is a company or another person.

Format. The guide word *Attention* is less common than other guide words and thus may have to be typed in later below the printed guide words. Use the same capitalization, punctuation, and spacing as that used for the other guide words. Leave at least one or two character spaces after the guide word and the colon (if any) before filling in the name of the designated person.

Follow the guidelines given earlier for an attention line in a letter. Although no punctuation is used after *Attention* in a letter, the same punctuation that follows all other guide words should follow *Attention* in a memo. Because space for preliminary material is usually more limited in a memo, the person's department may have to be typed on a separate line.

> **ATTENTION:** Sheila R. Bigelow
> Research Department

Subject Line

A subject line, summarizing the contents in a few words, is very important in a memo. Since a principal objective of a memo is to communicate quickly and informally, a subject line contributes significantly to this goal by focusing on and condensing the key topic.

Format. The guide word *Subject* is often the last guide word to appear in the collection that precedes the body of a memo. It is usually one of the words already printed on a standard memo but, if not, may be typed in later below all other guide words.

Use the same capitalization, punctuation, and spacing as that used for the other guide words. Leave at least one or two character spaces after the guide word and the colon (if any) before filling in the subject line.

Writing Style. Follow the style of writing described earlier for a subject line in a letter. Although a subject line may be written in all capitals, it is often styled the same as the other fill-in lines of a memo, with the major words capitalized.

> **SUBJECT:** SUPER VGA MONITOR

> **SUBJECT:** Super VGA Monitor

Body

The body of a memo is written in essentially the same way that the body of a letter is written. It should be composed in normal prose style, with good grammar and proper spelling, capitalization, and punctuation, as described in Chapter 2.

Format. Begin your message two to four line spaces below the last line of the guide-word material. Single-space the text and leave one line space between paragraphs. Some memo formats have ruled boxes to indicate the margins. If you are using regular business stationery without such lines, leave conventional margins of 1¼ to 2 inches. Paragraphs may be indented ½ to 1 inch but are usually typed flush left in a memo.

Writing Style. As suggested for your letters, avoid long, cumbersome sentences and paragraphs. Use techniques to simplify the text. Numbered lists, indented (blocked) examples, and tables, for example, will help to simplify complex discussions, a principal aim of a memo. Follow the rule for letter writing if the text is too long for one page: Put at least two lines of the body on the second page.

Signature Line

Most memos don't have signature lines, but a few styles provide a space for signing the memos, and any memo may be initialed, if desired.

Format. Some commercial memo formats have a ruled line at the bottom of the message area where the sender may sign the memo. Those that have both a message and a reply section may have two signature lines, one where the sender will sign and the other where the person replying will sign. Any handwritten signature in such cases must be consistent with the typed names of the addressee (after the guide word *To*) and the sender (after the guide word *From*). If a sender's name is typed as *Alvin A. Schneider*, for example, it should be signed exactly the same way, not as *A. A. Schneider*.

Most memos, however, have no designated signature line, and the memo is properly sent without a handwritten signature. Writers who object to this omission may pen their initials about two line spaces below the memo body, a little to the right of the center of the page, or near the typed name after the guide word *From*.

Identification Line

The identification line provides the same information in a memo as in a letter. It indicates who wrote or dictated, who signed or sent, and who transcribed or typed a message. The same person usually writes and sends the memo, but sometimes two people are involved.

Format. Place the identification line against the left margin two line spaces below the body of the letter or below any handwritten initials that have been penned below the body. Some firms prefer that the identification line appear only on file copies. Follow the rules described earlier for an identification line in a letter.

Enclosure Notation

The enclosure notation provides the same information in a memo as it gives in a letter. It tells the addressee what you are enclosing in the envelope along with your memo.

Format. Place the enclosure notation against the left margin, one or two line spaces below the identification line. The identification line, enclosure notation, and copy notation may all be single-spaced or double-spaced, depending on the length of the memo and available space.

Writing Style. Since most memos are sent domestically, the word *Enclosure* may be abbreviated as *Enc.* (Avoid abbreviations in international correspondence.) You can specify after the notation what is enclosed or how many items are enclosed. If you want any item returned, indicate that as well.

Refer to the examples of enclosure notations given earlier for a letter.

Mail Notation

The mail notation indicates how the memo was sent if it was mailed some way other than by interoffice delivery or regular first-class postal mail. Often this information is placed only on the sender's file copy.

Format. Place the notation against the left margin, one or two line spaces below the enclosure notation, depending on whether you are single- or double-spacing all notations.

> By Certified Mail
>
> By UPS Next-Day Air

Copy Notation

The copy notation indicates who will receive a copy of the memo other than the addressee.

Format. Place the copy notation against the left margin, one or two line spaces below the mail notation, depending on whether you are single- or double-spacing all notations.

Writing Style. The copy notation may be abbreviated or spelled out in domestic correspondence. Use the copy notations described and illustrated earlier for a letter.

Postscript

Like the postscript in a letter, the postscript in a memo is a brief comment that would be inappropriate in the memo body. Like all abbreviated material, the postscript should be avoided in international correspondence.

Format. Follow the same format described earlier for a postscript in a letter.

Continuation-Page Heading

Some memos are brief messages that don't warrant the use of full-size letterhead stationery; others, however, are mini-reports that require more than one page. When a memo requires two or more pages, each succeeding page must begin with a continuation-page heading the same as that used in a long letter.

Format. Follow the same format described earlier for a continuation-page heading in a letter.

Heading. The discussion of a continuation-page heading for a letter illustrates three common styles also appropriate for a memo.

Envelope

Interoffice memos are usually delivered by company clerks in interoffice envelopes or may be transmitted electronically, without the need for envelopes, through an interoffice or outside E-mail system.

Format. Interoffice envelopes commonly have a space on the outside for you to hand-write the addressee's name and department. Memos sent outside the office through the U.S. Postal Service or a private-delivery company must be addressed the same as an envelope containing a letter. The two common formats, illustrated in Section 58, are the traditional and OCR formats.

57. FORMS OF ADDRESS

The correct forms of address to use in the inside address and salutation of letters in domestic correspondence vary depending on the recipient's gender, official status, and personal familiarity with the writer. You wouldn't use *Dear Mrs. Cole* in a greeting to your best friend, and you wouldn't say *Dear Sally* in a greeting to a dignitary you've never met.

Unless someone is a close friend or a relative whom you always address by his or her first name, you should use the appropriate title with the person's last name. Always use the title *Dr.* (*Dear Dr. Windham*) rather than *Mr.*, *Mrs.*, or *Ms.* for someone who has earned a doctorate, unless you know that the person prefers a nonscholastic title. But never use a general job title (*Dear Business Manager Windham*) in the inside address or salutation.

The list of correct address forms in this section provides examples of the proper titles to use in the inside address and salutation of business and social correspondence. Consult a current book of etiquette or a secretarial handbook for rules about addressing governmental, judicial, military, religious, academic, and other officials.

The inside address to a person at work should include the individual's proper personal or professional title; the official name of the individual's place of employment, with department when pertinent; and the correct street address or post office box, city, two-letter state abbreviation, and zip code. Some writers omit the job title when it will cause an address to run over four lines, but often the job title and department are helpful in locating individuals in large companies. (Section 56 describes the use of academic degrees with a name, departmental and company titles, and other parts of the inside address.) All of the following forms are correct.

Dr. Walter B. Levinson, Manager
Samuels & Bernstein, Inc.
Legal Department
1111 North Avenue
Columbus, OH 43218-2158

Dear Dr. Levinson:

Dr. Walter B. Levinson, D.Com.L., D.Adm.
Manager, Legal Department
Samuels & Bernstein, Inc.
1111 North Avenue
Columbus, OH 43218-2158

Dear Dr. Levinson:

Dr. Walter B. Levinson, Manager
Ms. Hannah Stein, Assistant Manager
Samuels & Bernstein, Inc.
1111 North Avenue
Columbus, OH 43218-2158

Dear Dr. Levinson and Ms. Stein:

Names and Titles

A letter addressed to a friend or relative at home should use
the appropriate personal title (*Mr., Mrs.,* or *Ms.*), or the
scholastic title *Dr.* when applicable, on the envelope. Job titles
and company names are not used in the envelope addresses
of personal letters sent to individuals at home. In a personal
letter, the inside address is omitted on the letter itself. A
comma, rather than a colon, should follow the salutation in a
personal letter.

Dr. Walter B. Levinson [envelope address]
1300 Elm Street
Columbus, OH 43210

Dear Walt,

Ms. Hannah Stein
801 West Sycamore Drive
Columbus, OH 43209

Dear Hannah,

Some people like to have their scholastic degrees included
with their names. If more than one degree is used after an
addressee's name, place the degree pertaining to the person's
profession first. Omit titles before the name when a degree is
used that means the same thing, such as *Dr.* and *M.D.* But
another title, such as *Dean*, may be used with degrees.

Dr. Marion Beacher or Marion Beacher, M.D.
President Marion Beacher or
   President Marion Beacher, M.D., Ph.D.

A personal and professional title may also precede a name when certain initials, such as designations of military service or religious order, are used after it. Some initials or numerals, such as *Jr.* and *III*, are part of the name, and a title properly precedes the name when they are included. If *Esq.* (*Esquire*) follows the name of a prominent person, however, no other title should precede the name.

Father James Heiland, S.J.
Captain Paula Schifford, USAF
Mr. Donald Bennett Sr.
Jane Addison, Esq.

Different titles may be required with the names of addressees in foreign countries. Although in the United States job titles such as *Director* or *Architect* are not used preceding a name, in some countries such titles are used in place of *Mr.*, *Mrs.*, or *Miss*: *Dir. Eva Van Zant*.

The order of names may also differ in some countries. In Japan, for example, the family name may be stated first (*Mr. Hiroshi Hatano*), although some businesspeople in other countries are adopting a Western-style arrangement with the family name last (*Mr. Hatano Hiroshi*). Follow the customs of the particular country. For further information about customs that affect international correspondence, contact the U.S. Embassy in the country of interest or the appropriate country desk officer at the U.S. Department of Commerce. Travel guides, books on social and business customs, and other pertinent literature may be available in your local library.

The following examples represent generally correct forms of address. If you know that someone prefers another form, however, respect the person's wishes.

Address Forms for Men

Use *Dr.* if the person has a doctorate; otherwise use *Mr.*

> Dr./Mr. Charles A. Ratchet
> [Address]
>
> Dear Dr./Mr. Ratchet:

Address Forms for Women

The following forms apply to women in general social and business correspondence.

Single Women. In business and informal social situations, use *Dr.* if the person has a doctorate; otherwise use *Ms.*

> Dr./Ms. Sonya Harlson
> [Address]
>
> Dear Dr./Ms. Harlson:

In strictly formal correspondence, such as a formal invitation, use *Dr.* if the person has a doctorate; otherwise use *Miss* (traditional) or, if the woman prefers, *Ms.* (modern): *Dr./Miss/Ms. Sonya Harlson.*

Married or Widowed Woman. In business situations, use *Dr.* if the person has a doctorate; otherwise use *Ms.* or, if the woman prefers, *Mrs.*, with the person's first name and the last name she is using in business (maiden or married).

> Dr./Ms./Mrs. Sonya Harlson Benson
> [Address]
>
> Dear Dr./Ms./Mrs. Sonya Harlson Benson:

In strictly formal social correspondence, such as an invitation, use *Mrs.* with the first and last name of the person's husband (*Mrs. Milton K. Benson*), unless the woman has retained her maiden name. Then use *Dr.* or *Ms.* with her own first and last names (*Dr./Ms. Sonya Harlson*). In strict social usage, unlike business usage, a letter would never be addressed to *Mrs. Sonya Benson,* only to *Mrs. Milton K. Benson.* But see the explanation for divorced women. If the person has retained her maiden name, and you are addressing both her and her husband, include both names: *Mr. Milton K. Benson and Dr./Ms. Sonya Harlson.*

Divorced Woman. In business and informal social situations, use *Dr.* if the person has a doctorate; otherwise use *Ms.* with the person's first name and the last name she is using in business (maiden or former married name).

> Dr./Ms. Sonya Harlson
> [Address]
>
> Dear Dr./Ms. Harlson:

In strictly formal social correspondence, such as an invitation, the traditional option is to use *Mrs.* with the woman's maiden name and former married name but no first name (*Mrs. Harlson Benson*). The contemporary alternative is to use *Mrs.* with the person's own first name and her former husband's last name, if she has retained his name (*Mrs. Sonya Benson*). If a divorced woman prefers another option, however, respect her wishes.

Address Forms for Two or More Persons

In business situations, use individual titles and names for a man and a woman, two men, or two women, according to the rules just stated for men and women. If no job titles are given, list names in alphabetical order; otherwise the person of higher rank should be mentioned first. Also, if one person has a doctorate and the other does not, the one addressed as *Dr.* should be listed first.

Dr./Ms. Sonya Harlson
Dr./Mr. Charles A. Ratchet
[Address]

Dear Dr./Ms. Harlson and Dr./Mr. Ratchet:

In social correspondence, address an unmarried couple as just described for a business relationship. Address a married couple according to the last name the woman has adopted (maiden or married). Use *Dr.* for either or both parties as the case applies.

Mr. and Mrs. Milton K. Benson
[Address]

Dear Mr. and Mrs. Benson:

Dr. and Mrs. Milton K. Benson
[Address]

Dear Dr. and Mrs. Benson:

Drs. Milton K. and Sonya H. Benson
[Address]

Dear Drs. Benson:

Dr. Sonya H. and Mr. Milton K. Benson
[Address]

Dear Dr. and Mr. Benson:

Dr./Mr. Milton K. Benson and
Dr./Ms. Sonya Harlson
[Address]

Dear Dr./Mr. Benson and Dr./Ms. Harlson:

Address Forms with Gender Unknown

Omit the title when you have been unable to find out if a person is a man or a woman.

T. C. McCaffree
[Address]

Dear T. C. McCaffree:

Address Forms for Organizations:

Use the same inside address style for an organization as for an individual, but change the salutation to *Ladies and Gentlemen* for a company consisting of both men and women.

Olmen Corporation
[Address]

Ladies and Gentlemen:

If the firm consists of only men or women, such as a partnership owned by two men or two women, use *Gentlemen* alone or *Ladies* alone.

William A. Barnett Associates
[Address]

Gentlemen:

58. ENVELOPE FORMATS

Correspondence that is not transmitted electronically or delivered by mail clerks in special interoffice envelopes must be addressed according to the requirements of the U.S. Postal Service or the private-delivery service that is used. Private services often provide their own mailing labels that must be properly filled out and then affixed either to your envelopes or to those supplied by the particular service.

When specific labeling and addressing requirements do not exist, letter writers use one of two envelope formats: a traditional format or an optical-character-reader (OCR) format. The OCR format is required by the U.S. Postal Service for envelopes that will be read by its automated equipment.

Envelopes for most personal letters are still addressed traditionally. The traditional model in this section shows the return address in the upper left corner. Although this is characteristic in business, many social and personal letter writers prefer to put the return address on the back flap. This style is especially common when formal correspondence, such as an invitation, is being sent.

The following models are examples of a traditional envelope format and an OCR envelope format. Refer to Section 56 for a description of the required writing style for OCR mail and specific postal requirements for positioning the address block and other elements correctly on the face of an envelope.

Traditional envelope format:

[Return Address]   [Postage]

            Ms. Jennifer Eastman
            400 Charter Boulevard, Apt. 16
            Palm Coast, FL 32142

OCR envelope format:

```
[Return Address]                        [Postage]
ADDRESS CORRECTION REQUESTED
                                SPECIAL DELIVERY


            ABC:  0001-02-94
            JEFFERSON TRANSFER CO
            ATTN MR BF SIMPSON
            500 FIRST ST   RM 12
            SPRINGFIELD NJ 07081-9810
```

59. FORMAL CORRESPONDENCE FORMATS

The format for formal social and business correspondence, such as a wedding invitation or the announcement of a company's anniversary, differs significantly from the letter and memo formats, described in Section 55, that are used for informal correspondence. Formal correspondence must follow stricter wording and formatting guidelines, although various modern styles that depart from traditional forms are now common. (Refer to Section 54 for a description of the writing paper, and foldover paper and cards used in formal correspondence.)

Announcements and Invitations

Announcements and invitations are the two major categories of formal correspondence. This section provides several model formats of common formal announcements and invitations.

Printed and Commercial Forms. Printers have numerous samples of printed and engraved announcements and invitations, ranging from ultramodern to ultraconservative. Some invitations, both semiformal and informal, are handwritten and sent on commercial fill-in cards or foldover cards that can be purchased at stationery and office-supply stores.

Handwritten Forms. Although formal invitations are frequently printed or engraved, partially printed or engraved fill-in forms or completely handwritten forms are also proper for occasions such as an invitation to dinner. In the traditional formal style, a handwritten invitation is usually written in black ink on white, off-white, or cream paper, which may contain the sender's address or have the family crest printed on it. Even if an invitation is handwritten rather than printed or engraved, the wording should be the same as that of a printed or engraved invitation. (For more about the proper wording of formal correspondence, consult a current book of etiquette.)

Replies. Many people sending an invitation enclose a printed fill-in reply card for the recipient to use in responding. Or the sender may request that replies be made by telephone rather than writing. Both reply cards and telephone replies conveniently relieve the recipient of preparing a formal third-person handwritten reply.

If you are replying to a relative or close friend, though, you might want to include a warm personal note. If a reply card is used, it may be returned along with your personal note. Always mail replies to the person or persons named on the invitation or on the envelope of the reply card.

TRADITIONAL FORMAL BUSINESS ANNOUNCEMENT (PRINTED OR ENGRAVED)

William Charles Drexall

announces the opening of his office

for the practice of law

at

100 Oak Street

Jefferson, Massachusetts 02533

413-555-2000

MODERN FORMAL BUSINESS ANNOUNCEMENT (PRINTED)

Anne Foster-Sharpe

has opened a new store

SHARPE FASHIONS N'THINGS

and wants to welcome you to

200 Park Square Shopping Center

Twinsburg, Ohio 44087

216-555-3000

FORMAL SOCIAL ANNOUNCEMENT (PRINTED)

Eva Lindquist

(formerly Eva Lindquist-Stulberg)

has changed her address to

700 Mingus Boulevard South

Georgetown, Connecticut 06829

FORMAL BUSINESS INVITATION
(PRINTED OR ENGRAVED)

[logo]

Howard Eddison III

President and General Manager

cordially invites you to

cocktails

to celebrate the company's twentieth anniversary

Friday, February 14

5 to 7 p.m.

900 Highway 88

Little Rock

R.s.v.p. card enclosed

FORMAL SOCIAL INVITATION
(PRINTED OR ENGRAVED)

Miss Janet Cowan Koepke

Mr. Carlton I. Vengrow

request the pleasure of your company

at dinner

on Saturday, the fifth of August

at half past seven o'clock

400 Norton Lane

Foster City, California 94404

415-555-6000

R.s.v.p.

FORMAL SOCIAL OR BUSINESS REPLY: ACCEPT
(HANDWRITTEN)

Mr. and Mrs. David K. Shelby
accept with pleasure
Mr. Joel Handley's
kind invitation for dinner
on Saturday, the first of May
at eight o'clock

FORMAL SOCIAL OR BUSINESS REPLY: REGRET (HANDWRITTEN)

Mr. and Mrs. David H. Shelby
regret that they are unable to accept
Mr. Joel Handley's
kind invitation for dinner
on Saturday, the first of May

FORMAL SOCIAL OR BUSINESS REPLY: COMBINATION (HANDWRITTEN)

Mr. David K. Shelby
accepts with pleasure
Mr. Joel Handley's
kind invitation for dinner
Saturday, the first of May
eight o'clock
but regrets that
Mrs. Shelby
will be unable to attend

Appendix
Model Letters and Memos

Model letters and memos are provided here to illustrate an appropriate style and tone for the more than two dozen categories of correspondence described in Section 2 of Chapter 1. In composing your own messages, however, consider each reader and adapt your personal writing style to the requirements of each situation. For specific composition guidelines, refer to all of the sections in Chapter 4. For guidelines in composing international correspondence, refer to Chapter 6.

Section 55 has examples of alternative formats that can be used for personal, social, and business correspondence. The model formats indicate the proper position of the various parts of letters and memos, such as the date and subject line. Section 56 explains how to punctuate and capitalize the different parts in personal, social, and business correspondence. Notice, for example, in the following letters that a colon follows the salutation in business and social letters, whereas a comma follows the salutation in personal letters to family and friends.

ACKNOWLEDGMENTS

Dear Hollie:

Your information on trends in college
enrollment by age category just arrived. It's
perfect--just what I need for my presentation
at the July seminar.

I really appreciate your prompt reply, Hollie.
Many thanks.

Best regards,

ADJUSTMENTS

Ladies and Gentlemen:

NORA C. ALBERTSON, BEST STORES ACCOUNT
NO. 31-2111-5079

My November 10, 1995, statement includes a
charge of $27.98 on October 22 for a tool case.
However, the case was defective, and I returned
it to your Heberville store on October 26. I've
enclosed a copy of the credit slip.

Please send a corrected statement to reflect the
$27.98 credit of October 26. Thank you.

Sincerely,

ANNOUNCEMENTS

TO: All Service Representatives
FROM: Bill Watts, Service Manager

AUGUST MEETING

The next meeting of members of the Service Department will be on Monday, August 4, from 8 to 9 a.m. in the employee lounge. Coffee and breakfast rolls will be available.

We should be prepared to discuss scheduling for the fall servicing of humidifiers and heat pumps. If any other topics need to be considered, please let me know by August 3.

I would appreciate hearing from you right away if you're unable to attend. Thanks very much.

APOLOGIES

Dear Mrs. Crandall:

You are absolutely right! You paid an additional $8.50 for rush delivery of your January 3 order, but two of the items had to be back-ordered. We were therefore unable to process and ship your merchandise on a rush basis.

You are indeed entitled to a refund for that portion of your order, and our check for $8.50 is enclosed. Please accept my sincerest apologies for the mistake. I appreciate your bringing it to my attention.

Cordially yours,

APPOINTMENTS

Dear Mr. Grenelli:

Yes, I would be happy to prepare your income tax return again this year.

I am usually in my office from 9 to 11 a.m. and 1 to 5 p.m. weekdays. If you will telephone my secretary, Ms. Kline, at 555-1000, she will be happy to schedule a time for you to deliver your material. A sheet is enclosed listing the information we will need from you.

Thanks for calling on me again to help with your taxes. I appreciate your business and look forward to seeing you soon.

Best regards,

APPRECIATION

Dear Harry:

Thanks so much for your kind words about my election to the school board. I'm especially happy to know that you support my position on refinancing. With your help and that of others, I hope I can do some good.

Cordially,

COLLECTIONS

Dear Ms. Atkins:

We want to call your attention to the enclosed copy of our March 1 invoice for $198.99. This balance on your account is now sixty days overdue.

Since we have not heard from you, we assume that your records agree with ours and that the balance owed on your account is correct. If you have any reason to dispute the amount, please contact us immediately. If not, we urge you to send us your check right away before the unpaid balance affects your credit standing.

We will appreciate your cooperation, Ms. Atkins. Thank you.

Sincerely,

COMPLAINTS

Ladies and Gentlemen:

I am returning for a refund one set of five hundred National Heritage address labels. These labels were ordered from your catalog on June 21 and were paid for by my check no. 2301 for $12.98. Your catalog states that the unused portion of an order may be returned within ten days for a full refund if the customer is not satisfied.

The enclosed labels were advertised as peel-and-stick labels. But the adhesive material appears to be defective. It is very difficult to get the labels to adhere to the paper, and those that do stick tend to curl up and fall off within minutes.

Please send your refund check of $12.98 to Mrs. Benson Hersey, Jr., at the return address given at the top of this letter. Thank you.

Sincerely,

CONGRATULATIONS

Dear Mr. Pennyworth:

We at Watkins Press are delighted to send you our sincerest congratulations on the twentieth anniversary of the Southwest Gallery of Fine Art.

Your gallery has been an important part of our community for each of the twenty years since your opening on April 5, 1975. Like so many others, we have eagerly anticipated each new display and have benefited from the many ways your gallery has enriched our lives.

We have enjoyed and appreciated having you as a customer and are very pleased to wish you and the Southwest Gallery many more years of success and progress.

Cordially,

CREDIT

Dear Ms. Anderson:

In reply to your inquiry about Stanwell Cleaners, our experience has been fully satisfactory. It has paid all of our invoices on time during the five years in which we have serviced its equipment. Invoices have averaged $220 a month.

We are pleased to have Stanwell Cleaners as a reliable customer and are happy to acknowledge our satisfaction with the way it has maintained its account.

If I can answer any additional questions, please let me know.

Sincerely,

EXPLANATIONS

TO: Henry Eikenbury
FROM: Sheila Foster-Rowe

PRICE INCREASES

As I promised last week, here are the price changes for four of our products. We decided to decrease the cost of the first two items because our competition has regularly been running ads for both at a lower cost. However, we're increasing the price of the last two because demand has been increasing and our original pricing was based on a below-market-value introductory plan.

	Currently	September 1
Over-Door Video Rack	$25.98	$19.98
Porch Light Cover	9.98	5.98
Under-Bed Storage Box	4.98	7.98
Snack Trio Set	6.98	7.98

Since these changes are effective September 1, they should appear in the fall catalog. I'd appreciate seeing proofs of the new copy before it goes into print.

Thanks very much, Henry.

Follow-ups

Dear Bob:

Have you had an opportunity yet to think about adding another session to our spring-workshop program? Since we need to complete the program in a couple weeks, I'd appreciate receiving your ideas on this by Friday, July 19.

Thanks, Bob.

Best regards,

Goodwill

Dear Ms. Forrester:

It was a pleasure to work with you and your staff at the Community Center's Annual Auction. Setting up the fascinating displays was so interesting that we hated to see the assignment end.

To express our appreciation for your
confidence in us, Ms. Forrester, please accept
this framed color photograph of the auction in
progress. Sincerest thanks.

Cordially,

HOLIDAY WISHES

Dear Jim:

At the top of my list of things to be thankful
for this New Year is my good fortune to have
you as a friend and associate.

This is the fifth year you have been
running our Florida office, and I've enjoyed
and appreciated every minute since you first
joined our firm.

Sincerest wishes to you and your family for a
wonderful holiday season and a bountiful 1996.

All the best,

INQUIRIES

Ladies and Gentlemen:

Do you have any information on environmentally
safe products? If so, please send an order form, as
well as any free brochures or other literature. If
you have no material available, could you direct me
to another source?

Thank you very much.

Sincerely,

INSTRUCTIONS

TO: A-B SCAN Users
FROM: ScanMasters, Inc.

A-B SCAN VERSION 4.0 REVISION

A-B SCAN users who purchased A-B SCAN
software Version 4.0 before April 15 should
disregard the previous instructions supplied
with the instruction booklet and substitute the
following:

Installing the A-B SCAN Program

1. Insert the A-B SCAN Installation Disk into
   Drive A.

2. At the DOS prompt, type: a:install <Enter>.

3. Follow the on-screen instructions to
   complete the installation. You will be
   prompted to select a program directory
   and a temporary file directory.

4. After installation is completed, store the
   A-B SCAN disks in a safe place.

5. Reboot your computer: Press <Ctrl> + <Alt>
   + <Del> or turn the power off and on again
   to reboot.

You are now ready to begin scanning
documents using A-B SCAN. Turn to Chapter 2
for a quick tutorial.

INTRODUCTIONS

Dear Mr. Goldberg:

I'm happy to introduce Benjamin Shipley, our new representative on the West Coast. Ben has many years of experience with water-purification processes and equipment. He is well qualified to investigate and discuss your needs in this area, and I know you'll enjoy his friendly, helpful attitude.

Ben will call you on Monday, October 14, to arrange a convenient time to meet you personally, and he'll be happy to answer any questions you have at that time. If you need help in the meantime, however, you can reach him at 213-555-6102.

Cordially,

INVITATIONS

Dear Marilyn,

Would you be able to have lunch with Ellie and me on Friday, June 3? I'd like to have both of you be my guest at the Princeton Inn. We could meet in the cocktail lounge at noon.

Ellie and I thought it would be fun for all of us to get together again, and it would also give us a chance to talk about plans for the Fourth of July weekend.

Could you let me know by Tuesday whether you can come? I hope you can. It will be great to see you and hear about your new job.

Love,

ORDERS

Ladies and Gentlemen:

Please send me the following items from your general office-products catalog and charge them to my account number 253762.

One (1) TMZ-43217 deluxe magazine file	$ 6.15
Twelve (12) SMZ-80799 carbon film ribbons at $4.95 each	59.40
Two (2) HMZ-64555 diskette trays at $21.95 each	43.90

I would appreciate knowing if any of these items cannot be shipped in one week. Thank you.

PERSONNEL

TO: Harvey J. Wilton
FROM: Sam Steinberg

ANNUAL REVIEW: DAVID K. HERTER

Here is my annual personnel summary for David K. Herter. Detailed rating charts on job skills and personal characteristics are enclosed.

EDUCATION AND EXPERIENCE: Herter is a 1990 graduate of Washington Business College. He has four years' experience as a computer operator in the Data Processing Division.

JOB SKILLS AND ABILITIES: Herter has excellent skills in computer operations, particularly with accounting software. He has adequate abilities in office practices and procedures but lacks personal communication skills.

PERSONAL CHARACTERISTICS: Herter is neat, quiet, and polite but tends to prefer assignments where he can work alone. He is a careful and accurate worker and handles detail work exceptionally well. However, he appears to lack boldness and confidence in teamwork situations.

SUMMARY: Herter is highly effective in person-machine activities but is less skilled in matters involving human relations. I recommend that he continue working as a computer operator, with appropriate salary advancement within that category.

If you need any other information, Mr. Wilton, let me know.

PROPOSALS

Dear Jeff:

SALES STRATEGIES AT CONVENTIONS

I'd like to propose some strategies for sales-people that could make their attendance at conventions more productive. Some of the veteran salespeople use these strategies already, but the less experienced members of the staff might benefit from a few tips.

1. Develop an overall strategy before leaving for the convention.

2. Make specific appointments before leaving for the convention.

3. Keep an appointment calendar with you at all times.

4. Carry a briefcase full of samples at all times.

5. Have a good supply of business cards with you at all times.

6. Keep your name tag on at all times.

7. Sit in strategic locations during the meeting sessions.

8. Stand in strategic locations during coffee breaks and receptions.

9. Meet as many prospective customers as possible, anywhere, anytime.

10. Make notes on all prospects as soon as possible after meeting each one.

It might help to have a preconvention strategy meeting and give everyone a printout of these suggestions.

If you like this idea, Jeff, let me know, and I'll make the arrangements. Thanks.

RECOMMENDATIONS

TO WHOM IT MAY CONCERN:

It's a pleasure for me to comment on the excellent service we have received from Madison Answering and Reception Services.

Madison has provided operator answering services for us for six years, and we have regularly had good reports from our clients on the prompt, courteous treatment they have received from the operators. We have never failed to receive a message, and we have never failed to receive a hundred percent effort from the Madison staff.

I'm happy to recommend Madison Answering and Reception Services and believe you will be very pleased with the quality of the service.

Sincerely,

REFERENCES

Dear Ms. Santos:

Jonathan Quigley has applied for a personal loan from us and has given Brewster National Bank as a banking reference. His application gives two account numbers: 19064321 (checking) and 0800-563 (savings).

We would appreciate knowing how long he has had these accounts, what the balances average, and whether he has satisfactorily maintained the accounts.

Thank you for your help.

Sincerely,

REMINDERS

TO: Donna Anderson
FROM: Arnold Marchand, Jr.

ENTERTAINMENT COMMITTEE

I hope you're still planning to serve on the Entertainment Committee this year. We need your good ideas and experience in arranging social functions.

Donna, would you please call me at extension 2014 to confirm that you'll be joining the rest of us on the committee. We need to set up a meeting schedule and start working on this year's program of events.

Thanks much.

REQUESTS

Dear Ann:

While helping Timmy with his Science Fair project, I thought about your wonderful collection of NASA souvenirs. Is there any chance that you might be willing to lend them to the Science Fair as a display, February 1-3? They're so interesting, and you're the only person I know who has such a complete collection.

I realize that it's asking a lot for you to give them up even for three days. But the children would be so thrilled to see them. They would be in a locked glass case for protection.

Let me know what you think, Ann. Many thanks for considering it.

Best wishes,

SALES

Dear Computer Owner:

We promised you that we would make your word processing easier, and that's just what we've done with this new version of Writing Better 4.0! We hope you'll take time to read the enclosed brochure describing these exciting new one-step features:

- One-step table preparation
- One-step formatting
- One-step bulleting
- One-step print preview

These one-step features are only a few of the many innovations in Version 4.0. It's a word processing user's dream come true! Customers who are already using Version 4.0 are amazed at its time-saving features. The best part is that 4.0 is designed to run on most computers in use today.

Don't wait! Use the enclosed card and send in your order now--while the price remains a low $329. Users of Version 3.1 can upgrade for only $75.

Sincerely,

SYMPATHY

Dear Bill,

I was so sorry to learn about your father's death. You and your family have my deepest sympathy.

Do let me know, Bill, if I can help in any way.

With love and sympathy,

THANKS

Dear Shirley,

What a lovely bouquet of garden flowers--and my favorite colors! It arrived this morning with your thoughtful note.

Thank you, Shirley, for the beautiful flowers and all your good wishes. I think I'm feeling better already!

Always,

Index